Henry George Spaulding

Sunday School Service Book and Hymnal

Henry George Spaulding

Sunday School Service Book and Hymnal

ISBN/EAN: 9783337089955

Printed in Europe, USA, Canada, Australia, Japan

Cover: Foto ©Thomas Meinert / pixelio.de

More available books at **www.hansebooks.com**

THE

SUNDAY SCHOOL

SERVICE BOOK

AND

HYMNAL.

Compiled and Edited

BY REV. HENRY G. SPAULDING.

SECRETARY OF THE UNITARIAN S. S. SOCIETY.

BOSTON:
UNITARIAN SUNDAY SCHOOL SOCIETY
1885.

PREFACE.

IN preparing these SERVICES the Editor has had the valuable counsel and assistance of the Publication Committee of the Unitarian Sunday School Society. The aim has been to provide Sunday School Services varied in structure and rich in liturgical and musical forms. They have been compiled for the use of schools which are wedded to no exclusive methods of conducting their worship, and which will claim and exercise great freedom of selection.

By having one hymn printed in its proper place in several of the Services, it is made practicable to go through the Service to the final singing without turning to the Hymnal or opening another book for a suitable hymn to be sung. In a few of the Services suggestions are offered to the superintendent with reference to additional Scripture lessons. Similar readings might be made a regular part of every Service. On the other hand, in schools where brevity is desired, the shorter Services may be used, or portions of the longer Services omitted; but it is earnestly recommended that each school become familiar with such Services as are chosen for use. Frequent repetition of a Service is necessary, in order that the responses, both verbal and musical, may be well rendered; and also that around familiar words and well-known melodies associations may cluster which shall kindle the glow of devotion. A single Service might be used to advantage once, or even twice, each month of the school year.

The Infant-Class Services — two of which have been arranged from Services already in use — are designed to provide the pupils in the primary department with simpler exercises specially adapted to their needs. A series of Infant-Class Songs, to be used in connection with these Services, will be found in the Hymnal.

The reverent attention of all — pupils and teachers — should be given to every service, that worship in the Sunday School may be a united offering of joyful praise and heartfelt prayer.

TABLE OF CONTENTS.

Opening Services.

No.		Page
1.	Joyful Confidence	1
2.	Trust	5
3.	The Eternal Goodness	8
4.	God in Nature	11
5.	Good Works	14
6.	Adoration	17
7.	The Law of Love	19
8.	Wisdom	21
9.	Moral Courage	24
10.	The Teachings of Jesus	28
11.	Life Eternal	33
12.	God our Life	35
13.	"Who forgiveth all thy Sins"	38
14.	Following after the Spirit of Jesus	41
15.	The Blessed Life	44
16.	God ever Present	48
17.	Worship	50

Closing Services.

First	52
Second	53
Third	54
Fourth	56

Special Services.

No.		Page
1.	Anniversary	58
2.	In Memoriam	62
3.	National	65
4.	Harvest	68
5.	Christmas	73
6.	Easter	79
7.	Floral	83
8.	Christening	86

Infant-Class Services.

First	88
Second	91
Third	93

HYMNS IN THE SERVICES.

Index of First Lines.

	PAGE
All our sinful words and ways	38
Bless'd are the pure in heart	44
Can a little child like me?	90
Careful Gard'ner, Friend so dear!	88
Courage, brother! do not stumble!	26
Day by day we magnify Thee	17
Do Thou, O Lord, in Thy dear love	16
Father and Friend, Thy light, Thy love	8
Father, gracious Father!	33
For mercies past we praise Thee, Lord	55
God the Father loves the children	89
Heavenly Shepherd, who art feeding	85
Holy God, we praise Thy name	21
How sweetly flowed the Gospel's sound	41
In pleasant lands have fallen the lines	65
In this hallowed dwelling	60
O Father, grace and virtue grant!	14
Oh, I love to think of Jesus as he sat beside the sea	28
Oh, happy is the man who hears	22
Oh, praise the Lord! sing praises to our God	1
Our Father, by whose grace we're called	24
Our Heavenly Father, Nature's mighty Ruler!	11
The King of Love my Shepherd is	62
Though faint, yet pursuing, we go on our way	35
We sing the mighty power of God	12
We worship Thee, sweet Will of God	19
Wherever He may guide me	3

SERVICES

FOR

THE SUNDAY SCHOOL.

First Service.

JOYFUL CONFIDENCE.

I. Introductory Sentences.

OH, magnify the Lord with me, and let us exalt His name together! With Him is the fountain of life, and in His light shall we see light. Trust in Him at all times.

Pour out your heart before Him. God is a refuge for us.

II. Anthem of Praise.

Oh, praise the Lord! sing praises to our God, Our Father and our Friend! O let our thoughts and thanks arise As grateful incense to the skies! Praise ye the Lord!

2 Praise ye the Lord! Sing praises to our
  Our Father and our Friend!   [God,
  Here may we prove the power of prayer
  To strengthen faith and sweeten care;
      Praise ye the Lord!

3 Praise ye the Lord! Sing praises to our
  Our Father and our Friend!   [God,
  May trusting faith and holy love
  Rise fervent to the throne above;
      Praise ye the Lord!

4 Praise ye the Lord!   Sing praises to our God,
   Our Father and our Friend!
   So let our life on earth be given
   To truth, to duty, and to heaven;
     Praise ye the Lord!

III. RESPONSIVE READING.

THE Lord is my light and my salvation; whom shall I fear?
   The Lord is the strength of my life; of whom shall I be afraid?
My heart trusted in Him, and I am helped.
Therefore, my heart greatly rejoiceth, and with my song will I praise Him.
The eyes of the Lord are upon the righteous, and His ears are open unto their cry.
The Lord is good unto them that wait for Him, to the soul that seeketh Him.
In all thy ways acknowledge Him, and He shall direct thy paths.
The Lord is nigh unto all them that call upon Him, to all that call upon Him in truth.
The Lord is good, a stronghold in the day of trouble.
Our soul waiteth for the Lord; He is our help and shield.
Cast thy burden upon the Lord, and He shall sustain thee.
If God is for us, who can be against us?
I waited patiently for the Lord, and He inclined unto me and heard my cry.
And He hath put a new song in my mouth, even praise unto our God.

IV. GLORIA.

Glo - ry, glo - ry, glo - ry be to Thee, O Lord!

V. RESPONSIVE READING.

I HAVE learned in whatsoever state I am therewith to be content.
   Be not therefore anxious for the morrow.
Be not anxious for your life what ye shall eat or what ye shall drink; nor yet for your body what ye shall put on
   Is not the life more than the food, and the body than the raiment?

Are not five sparrows sold for two farthings, and not one of them is forgotten before God?
Fear not, therefore: ye are of more value than many sparrows.
Thou art careful and troubled about many things; but one thing is needful, —
Have faith in God.
When thou saidst, Seek ye my face, my heart said unto thee, Thy face, Lord, will I seek.

ALL SING.

Wher-ev-er He may guide me, No want shall turn me back;

My Shep-herd is be-side me, And noth-ing can I lack.

I had fainted unless I had believed to see the goodness of the Lord in the land of the living.

ALL SING:

The storm may beat upon me,
My heart may low be laid;
But God is round about me,
And can I be dismayed?

When my father and my mother forsake me, then the Lord will take me up.

ALL SING:

His wisdom ever waketh,
His sight is never dim;
He knows the way He taketh,
And I will walk with Him.

VI. Prayer.

O LORD, our heavenly Father, we bring to Thee, in this quiet hour, an offering of love, of gratitude, and of praise. We bless Thee that Thou givest us all things richly to enjoy. We thank Thee for minds to know, and hearts to love, Thee, and for the pure affections that bind us to one another. We praise Thee for Thy word so clearly shown to us, and for Thy spirit, which is always near and ready to help us. May we walk in the light of Thy truth and find our highest joy in doing Thy blessed will! Make us faithful to each day's nearest duties, and lead us kindly on through life's uncertain scenes to our eternal home. We ask it for Thy mercy's sake. AMEN.

VII. Hymn.

Second Service.

TRUST.

I. INTRODUCTORY SENTENCES.

MY soul, rest thou on God alone; for from Him cometh my help.
He alone is my rock and my salvation. He is my safeguard: I shall not fall.
From God cometh my help and my glory. My strong rock, my refuge, is God.

II. ANTHEM OF PRAISE.

Oh, praise the Lord! sing prais-es to our God, Our Fa-ther and our Friend! O let our thoughts and thanks a-rise As grate-ful in-cense to the skies! Praise ye the Lord!

2 Praise ye the Lord! Sing praises to our
Our Father and our Friend! [God,
Here may we prove the power of prayer
To strengthen faith and sweeten care;
    Praise ye the Lord!

3 Praise ye the Lord! Sing praises to our
Our Father and our Friend! [God,
May trusting faith and holy love
Rise fervent to the throne above;
    Praise ye the Lord!

4 Praise ye the Lord! Sing praises to our God,
   Our Father and our Friend!
   So let our life on earth be given
   To truth, to duty, and to heaven;
     Praise ye the Lord!

III. Responses.

Father Almighty, bless us with Thy blessing,
Answer in love Thy children's supplication;

Hear Thou our prayers, the spoken and unspoken:
   Hear us, our Father!

Shepherd of souls, who bringest all who seek Thee
To pastures green beside the peaceful waters;

Tenderest Guide, in ways of cheerful duty
   Lead us, Good Shepherd!

Spirit of Mercy, from Thy watch and keeping
No place can part, nor hour of time remove us;

Give us Thy good, and save us from our evil,
   Infinite Spirit!

IV. Gloria.

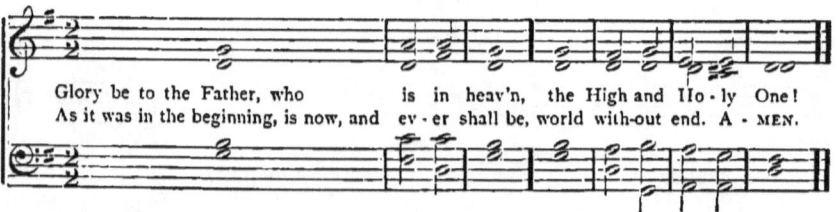

Glory be to the Father, who is in heav'n, the High and Ho-ly One!
As it was in the beginning, is now, and ev-er shall be, world with-out end. A-MEN.

V. Responsive Reading.

Bless the Lord, O my soul; and all that is within me, bless His holy name.
  Bless the Lord, O my soul, and forget not all His benefits.
Who redeemeth thy life from destruction;
  Who crowneth thee with loving kindness and tender mercies.

Like as a father pitieth his children, so the Lord pitieth them that fear Him.

The Lord is my shepherd: I shall not want.

He maketh me to lie down in green pastures: He leadeth me beside the still waters.

He restoreth my soul: He leadeth me in the paths of righteousness for His name's sake.

Yea, though I walk through the valley of the shadow of death, I will fear no evil; ‘

For Thou art with me: Thy rod and Thy staff they comfort me.

Thou anointest my head with oil: my cup runneth over.

Surely, goodness and mercy shall follow me all the days of my life; and I will dwell in the house of the Lord forever.

VI. GLORIA.

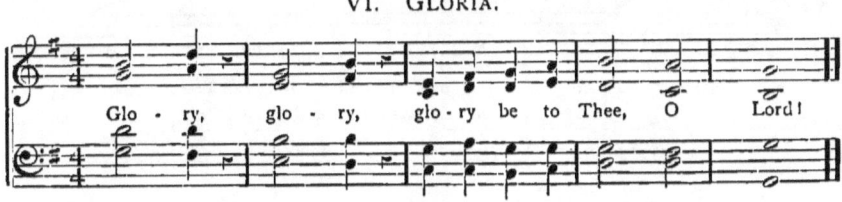

Glo - ry, glo - ry, glo - ry be to Thee, O Lord!

VII. PRAYER.

FATHER, in the spirit of the children of Thy love, we would feel Thy presence with us now. Each day Thou hast gone out and come in with us. Every morning has brought a blessing; every evening has told us of Thy care. We would always walk in the light of Thy love. We would be sure that Thou wilt ever help us, to keep us from wrong and evil, and to lead us in the ways of goodness and truth. As we give ourselves into Thy kind care, may we be content to feel that Thy hand is holding us up, and Thine arm supporting us always. Thus may we go forward through our life on earth. Growing ever more and more in grace and in goodness, may we be ready to enter upon the blessed life in heaven, when Thou shalt call us hence. AMEN.

VIII. HYMN.

Third Service.

THE ETERNAL GOODNESS.

I. Introductory Sentences.

O THAT men would praise the Lord for His goodness, and for His wonderful works to the children of men!

The Lord is good to all, and His tender mercies are over all His works.

Thy kingdom, O God, is an everlasting kingdom; and Thy dominion endureth through all generations.

II. Metrical Chant.

1. Father and Friend, Thy light, Thy love, Beaming through all Thy works we see;
Thy glory gilds the heav'ns above, And all the earth is full of Thee. A-MEN.

After Verse 4.

2 We know not in what hallow'd part
   Of the wide heav'ns Thy throne may be;
   But this we know, — that where Thou art,
   Strength, wisdom, goodness, dwell with Thee.

3 Thy children shall not faint nor fear,
   Sustain'd by this delightful thought, —
   Since Thou, their God, art everywhere,
   They cannot be where Thou art not.

4 Then from our lips shall ever ring
   Glad strains in honor of our King;
   To Thee, our Father, will we sing
   An endless Alleluia. AMEN.

III. Responsive Reading.

THOU, O Lord, art a God full of compassion, and gracious; long-suffering, and plenteous in mercy and truth.
Show us Thy mercy, O Lord, and grant us Thy salvation.
Whom have I in heaven but Thee?
And there is none upon earth that I desire beside Thee.
My flesh and my heart fail;
But God is the strength of my heart, and my portion forever.
For Thou, Lord, art good, and ready to forgive;
And plenteous in mercy to all them that call upon Thee.
Return unto thy rest, O my soul, for the Lord hath dealt bountifully with thee.
For his merciful kindness is great toward us.

IV. Gloria.

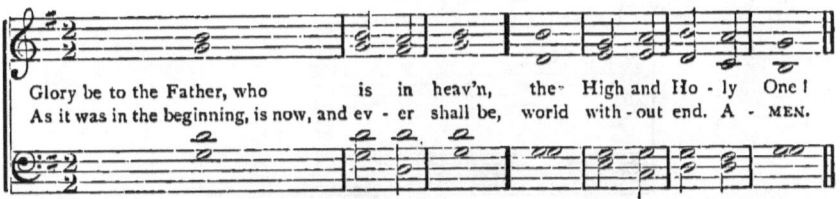

Glory be to the Father, who is in heav'n, the High and Ho-ly One!
As it was in the beginning, is now, and ev-er shall be, world with-out end. A-MEN.

V. Responses.

O GIVE thanks unto the Lord, for He is good:

ALL SING.

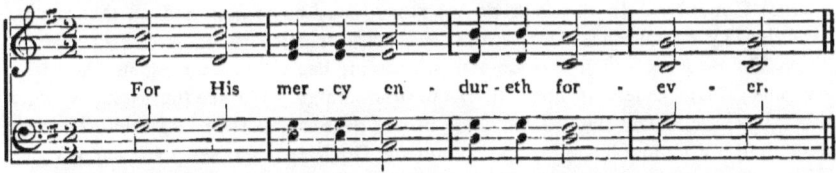

For His mer-cy en-dur-eth for-ev-er.

To Him that by wisdom made the heavens; that stretched out the earth above the waters.

ALL SING.— For His mercy endureth forever.

To Him that made great lights,— the sun to rule by day; the moon and stars to rule by night.

ALL SING.— For His mercy endureth forever.

Who doeth wonderful works to the children of men.

ALL SING.— For His mercy endureth forever.

Who made His people to go forth like sheep, and guided them in the wilderness like a flock; who brought them out of darkness and the shadow of death, and broke their bands in sunder.

ALL SING. — For His mercy endureth forever.

Who raiseth up the poor out of the dust, and saveth them that cry unto Him in their trouble.

ALL SING. — For His mercy endureth forever.

Who remembereth us in our low estate; who is our sun and our shield.

ALL SING. — For His mercy endureth forever.

VI. PRAYER.

O THOU, who art the Father of all spirits and the giver of all good, in thanks beyond what words can speak, we would here adore Thee. Thou art the Eternal Goodness. In this faith do we rest. Over all that is and all that can be, extends Thy conquering love. From Thy spirit which sustains us we cannot go. From Thy presence which surrounds us we cannot flee. Thou turnest us back from our sins; Thou callest us home from our wanderings. We see the wrong which is around us; we lament the evil which is in our hearts. But we know that Thou art good, and we cannot measure Thy power or Thy love. We see the pain and loss which abound in the world; but we also hear the words of blessing which Jesus spoke. We think of him as he lived on the earth, when he went about doing good. We hear his prayer of forgiveness upon the cruel cross. O Thou who art his God and our God, help us to lean our hearts on Thee. May we be sure that no harm can ever come from Thee to us; that we, Thy children, can never go beyond the reach of Thy love and Thy care. And so trusting Thee, loving Thee, and doing Thy will, may we be indeed Thine for evermore. AMEN.

VII. HYMN.

Fourth Service.

GOD IN NATURE.

I. HYMN.

1. Our Heav'n-ly Fa-ther, Na-ture's might-y Rul-er! Humbly before Thee bow we down! Thee will we ev-er love, Ev-er will hon-or Thee, Who art our glo-ry, joy, and crown.

2   Fair are the meadows,
    Fairer still the woodlands,
  Robed in the blooming garb of Spring;
    Thou, God, art fairer,
    Thou, Lord, art purer,
  Who makest every glad heart sing.

3   Bright is the sunshine,
    Softly fall the moonbeams,
  Splendor arrays the starry host;
    Thou, God, art brighter,
    Thou, Lord, art purer
  Than all the orbs that heav'n can boast.

4   Fair are the summer flowers,
    Fairer still are children
  Wearing youth's bloom upon the heart;
    Yet flow'rs must perish,
    Death will its harvest reap,
  And Thou, alone, eternal art.

II. Responsive Reading.

BLESS the Lord, O my soul! O Lord, my God, thou art very great.
Thou art clothed with glory and majesty.
Thou coverest thyself with light, as with a garment; thou stretchest out the heavens like a curtain.
Thou makest the clouds thy chariot, and ridest upon the wings of the wind.
Thou makest the winds thy messengers, the flaming lightnings thy ministers.
O Lord! how manifold are Thy works! In wisdom hast Thou made them all.
The invisible things of God since the creation of the world are clearly seen, being perceived through the things that are made.
He maketh his sun to rise on the evil and the good; and sendeth rain on the just and the unjust.
Consider the lilies of the field, how they grow: they toil not, neither do they spin.
Yet God doth clothe the grass of the field.
Behold the birds of the air, that they sow not, neither do they reap nor gather into barns.
Yet your Heavenly Father feedeth them.
Are not two sparrows sold for a farthing?
Yet not one of them shall fall to the ground without your Father.

III. Chant.

We sing the might-y pow'r of God, That made the moun-tains rise;
That spread the flowing seas a-broad, And built the lof-ty skies.

2 We sing the wisdom' that or'dain'd
　　The sun to rule the day,
　　The moon shines full at' His com'mand,
　　And all the stars obey.

3 We sing the goodness' of the' Lord,
　　That fill'd the earth with food ;
　　He form'd the creatures' with His' word
　　And then pronounced them good.

4 There 's not a plant or' flow'r be'low
　　But makes Thy glories known ;
　　And clouds arise and' tempests' blow
　　By order from Thy throne.

IV. Scripture Readings by the Superintendent.

Selections from the Psalms [Ps. xix. 1–6 ; cxlvii. 7–9, 12–18 ; and cxlviii. 1–13] ; or Job, chapter xxxviii.

V. Prayer.

O THOU, whom no eye can see, but every heart may feel : in lowly prayer we come to Thee. May Thy pure spirit teach us what we ought to ask. We thank Thee for this fair earth on which we live, and for the shining sky above our heads. All the things which Thou hast made tell us of Thy power ; they speak to us of Thy wisdom ; they show us how kind and good Thou art. We thank Thee, too, for all our friends ; for all who have taught us Thy truth ; and for those who have touched our hearts with the sense of Thy tender love. May Thy great truths be as a lamp unto our feet. May love that shall be a little like Thy pure love, shine forth from all our lives. As we work and as we play, may we rejoice in the Lord, and seek to do His holy will. AMEN.

VI. Hymn.

Fifth Service.

GOOD WORKS.

I. Introductory Sentences.

THUS speaketh the Lord of Hosts, saying, Execute true judgment, and show compassion every man to his neighbor.

Seeing that the love of God is never standing idle, so be ye constantly abounding in good works for His sake.

The grand deciding question at the last day will be, not what have you said or what have you believed, but what have you done?

Be ye doers of the word, and not hearers only. For not the hearers of the law are just before God, but the doers of the law shall be justified.

II. Versicle.

ALL SING.   MENDELSSOHN.

O Father, grace and virtue grant! No more we wish, no more we want:
To know, to serve Thee, and to love, Is peace below, is bliss above.

III. Responsive Reading.

WHEREWITH shall I come before the Lord, and bow myself before the Most High God?

He hath showed thee, O man, what is good.

And what doth the Lord require of thee but to do justly, and to love mercy, and to walk humbly before thy God?

Mercy is better than sacrifice.

Pure religion and undefiled before our God and Father is this:
To visit the fatherless and widows in their affliction, and to keep himself unspotted from the world.
If any man among you seem to be religious and bridleth not his tongue, this man's religion is vain.
Speak ye every man the truth to his neighbor.
Let all bitterness and wrath and clamor and evil-speaking be put away from you, with all malice.
And be ye kind to one another, tender-hearted, forgiving one another.
Be ye therefore imitators of God, as beloved children. Walk in love, and walk as children of light.
For the fruit of the light is in all goodness, and righteousness, and truth.
Add to your faith, virtue; and to virtue, knowledge; and to knowledge, temperance; and to temperance, patience; and to patience, godliness; and to godliness, brotherly kindness; and to brotherly kindness, love.

IV. Versicle.

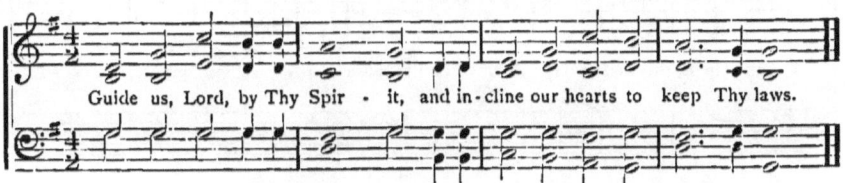

Guide us, Lord, by Thy Spirit, and incline our hearts to keep Thy laws.

V. Responsive Reading.

WHAT doth it profit if a man say he hath faith, but have not works? Can that faith save him?
As the body apart from the spirit is dead, even so faith apart from works is dead.
But some one will say, Thou hast faith, and I have works: show me thy faith apart from thy works, and I by my works will show thee my faith.
Let us not love in word, neither with the tongue, but in deed and truth.
The fruit of the spirit is love, joy, peace, long-suffering, kindness, goodness, faithfulness, meekness, temperance.
As we have opportunity, let us work that which is good toward all men.
In love of the brethren, be tenderly affectioned one to another;
In honor preferring one another.
Rejoice with them that rejoice; weep with them that weep.
If it be possible, as much as in you lieth, be at peace with all men.

Render to no man evil for evil: but if thine enemy hunger, feed him; if he thirst, give him drink.

Be not overcome of evil, but overcome evil with good.

Whatsoever things are true, whatsoever things are honorable, whatsoever things are just, whatsoever things are pure, whatsoever things are lovely, whatsoever things are of good report, — if there be any virtue, and if there be any praise, think on these things.

VI. VERSICLE.

ALL SING.　　　　　　　　　　　　　　　　　　　　　　　　　MENDELSSOHN.

Do Thou, O Lord, in Thy dear love, Fit us for per-fect rest a-bove;

And help us, this and ev'-ry day, To live more near-ly as we pray. A-MEN.

VII. PRAYER.

O GOD our Father, good and kind, though we forget Thee, Thou dost never forget us. Thou makest the sun to shine, and the rain to fall, and givest us all the blessings we enjoy. Thou hast given us the dear friends whom we love, and who love us; all the joys of this fair world we live in, and all the bright hopes of the better life. What shall we render unto Thee for all Thy benefits? May we bring Thee pure and grateful hearts. May we do justly, love mercy, and walk humbly before Thee. May we love Thee truly, and show Thee our love by doing our duty cheerfully; by loving all around us, and helping all whom we have power to help. So may we grow wiser and better every day. Bless us, we pray Thee, and those who are dear to us, and all Thy children everywhere. May all know and love Thee, and serve and worship Thee, in spirit and in truth. AMEN.

VIII. HYMN.

Sixth Service.

ADORATION.

I. Reading and Responses.

OH, come, let us sing unto the Lord; let us heartily rejoice in the strength of our salvation.

ALL SING.

Day by day we mag-ni-fy Thee; When, as each new day is born, In our hap-py homes we bless Thee For the mer-cies of the morn. A-MEN.

Let us come before His presence with thanksgiving, and show ourselves glad in Him with psalms.

ALL SING. [Music as before.]
> Day by day we magnify Thee,
> When our hymns in school we raise;
> Daily work begun and ended
> With the daily voice of praise.

Let your light shine before men, that they may see your good works and glorify your Father who is in heaven.

ALL SING. [Music as before.]
> Day by day we magnify Thee,
> Not in words of praise alone;
> Truthful lips and meek obedience
> Show Thy glory in Thine own.

Then shall the king say, Come, ye blessed of my Father, inherit the kingdom prepared for you from the foundation of the world.

ALL SING. [Music as before.]

   Day by day we magnify Thee, —
    Till our days on earth shall cease ;
   Till we rest from mortal labors,
    And enjoy eternal peace. AMEN.

II. RESPONSIVE READING.

BLESSED art Thou, O Lord.
 Teach us Thy statutes.
Open Thou our eyes, that we may behold wondrous things out of Thy law.
Deal bountifully with Thy servants, that we may live and keep Thy word.
Blessed is the man whom Thou choosest ;
Whose heart inclines to Thy ways.
With my whole heart have I sought Thee.
Oh, let me not wander from Thy commandments.
Be ye therefore imitators of God, as beloved children ; and walk in love, as Christ also hath loved us, and hath given himself for us. And grieve not the Holy Spirit of God. Let all bitterness and wrath and anger and clamor and evil-speaking be put away from you, with all malice. And be ye kind one to another, tender-hearted, forgiving one another.

III. PRAYER.

GRACIOUS God, our heavenly Father, we bless Thee that we may all be taught of Thee ; that, in our lack of wisdom, we may come to Thee for a full supply. We are met to study Thy truth. Give us a meek and teachable spirit, that we may be instructed out of Thy living word. While we listen to what is spoken in our outward ears, may we also hear and obey that still, small voice which ever speaks within our souls. May Thy heavenly kingdom come, and may Thy blessed will be done by us on earth as it is done by the perfect ones above ; that so we may be true disciples and faithful followers of our Master, Jesus Christ. AMEN.

IV. HYMN.

Seventh Service.

THE LAW OF LOVE.

I. INTRODUCTORY SENTENCES.

WITH my whole heart have I sought Thee. Oh, let me not wander from Thy commandments.

Teach me, O Lord, the way of Thy statutes; and I shall keep it unto the end.

II. READING AND RESPONSES.

JESUS said, The first of all the commandments is: Hear, O Israel, the Lord our God is one Lord; and thou shalt love the Lord thy God with all thy heart, and with all thy soul, and with all thy mind, and with all thy strength. This is the first commandment.

ALL SING.

We worship Thee, sweet will of God, And all Thy ways adore;
And ev'ry day we live we long To love Thee more and more.

And the second is like unto it: Thou shalt love thy neighbor as thyself. On these two commandments hang all the law and the prophets.

ALL SING. [Music as before.]

How sweet, how heavenly,' is the sight,
When those who love the Lord
In one another's' peace delight,
And thus fulfil His word!

A new commandment I give unto you, that ye love one another; even as I have loved you, that ye also love one another. By this shall all men know that ye are my disciples, if ye have love one to another.

ALL SING. [Music as before.]
   Love is the golden' chain that binds
    The happy souls above;
   And he's an heir of' heaven that finds
    His bosom glow with love.

Therefore, all things whatsoever ye would that men should do to you, do ye even so to them; for this is the law and the prophets.

ALL SING. [Music as before.]
   Then, Jesus, be thy' spirit ours;
    And swift our feet shall move
   To deeds of pure self' sacrifice,
    And the sweet tasks of love.

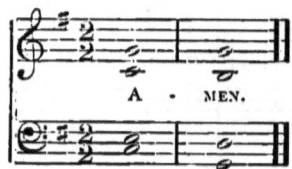

III. SCRIPTURE READING BY SUPERINTENDENT.

[1 Cor. xiii.; or, 1 John iv. 7-19.]

IV. PRAYER.

OUR Father who art in heaven, may we love and obey Thee. May we seek to enter into Thy kingdom by doing Thy will; by kindness and patience; by justice and truthfulness; by loving each other, and loving all, even those who are unkind to us. Send into our hearts Thy holy spirit of peace and good-will. Forgive us our sins as we forgive those who injure us. Help us as we study Thy truth. May we love it and live by it. Keep us from sin and from all evil, now and always. We ask it as disciples of Jesus. AMEN.

V. HYMN.

Eighth Service.

WISDOM.

I. Introductory Sentences.

THEY that put their trust in the Lord shall understand the truth: for grace and mercy are to His saints; and His word preserveth them that put their trust in Him.

The desire of wisdom bringeth to a kingdom;

For wisdom is the brightness of the everlasting light, the unspotted mirror of the energy of God, and the image of His goodness.

II. Te Deum Laudamus.

FROM A GERMAN MELODY.

Ho-ly God, we praise Thy name; Lord of all, we bow before Thee;
All on earth Thy scep-tre claim; All in heav'n a-bove a-dore Thee:
In-fi-nite Thy vast do-main; Ev-er-last-ing is Thy reign.

III. Responsive Reading.

WISDOM is glorious, and never fadeth away:
Yea, she is easily seen of them that love her, and found of such as seek her.
Whoso seeketh her early shall have no great labor; for he shall find her sitting at his doors:
For she goeth about seeking such as are worthy of her, and meeteth them in every thought:
For she is the breath of the power of God, and a pure influence flowing from the glory of the Almighty;
In all ages entering into holy souls, she maketh them friends of God, and prophets.
For the very true beginning of wisdom is the desire of discipline;
And the care of discipline is love.
The word of God most high is the fountain of wisdom; and her ways are everlasting habitations.
To fear the Lord is the beginning of wisdom.
To fear the Lord is fulness of wisdom, and filleth men with her fruits.
If thou desire wisdom, keep the commandments, and the Lord shall give her unto thee.
Blessed is the man that doth meditate good things in wisdom, and that reasoneth of holy things by his understanding.
Blessed is he whose conscience hath not condemned him, and who has not fallen from the way of the Lord.

IV. Metrical Chant.

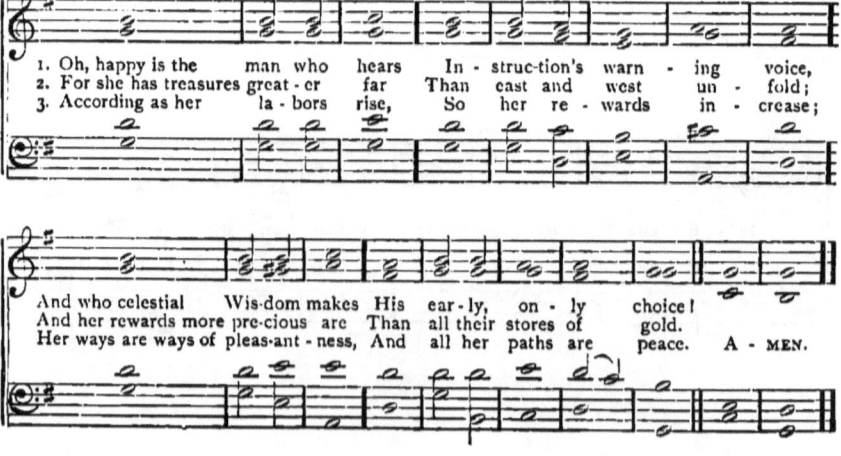

1. Oh, happy is the man who hears In-struction's warn-ing voice,
2. For she has treasures great-er far Than east and west un-fold;
3. According as her la-bors rise, So her re-wards in-crease;

And who celestial Wis-dom makes His ear-ly, on-ly choice!
And her rewards more pre-cious are Than all their stores of gold.
Her ways are ways of pleas-ant-ness, And all her paths are peace. A-MEN.

V. Prayer.

O GOD of our fathers and Lord of mercy, who hast made all things with Thy word! give us that wisdom which is the brightness of the everlasting light and the image of Thine own goodness, — the wisdom which is more beautiful than the sun, and above all the order of the stars, and being compared with the light, is found before it. For we Thy servants are but feeble, and too young to understand judgments and laws. For what man can think what the will of the Lord is? Thy counsel who hath known, except Thou give wisdom, and send Thy Holy Spirit from above? O God, in mercy Thou orderest all things. Thou lovest all the things that are, and abhorrest nothing which Thou hast made. Even if we sin we are Thine, knowing Thy power; but we will not sin, knowing that we are counted Thine. So shall our works be acceptable unto Thee, O Lord, thou Lover of Souls! AMEN.

VI. Hymn.

Ninth Service.

MORAL COURAGE.

I. Introductory Sentences.

BE of good courage, and He shall strengthen your heart,
All that hope in the Lord.

> So nigh is grandeur to our dust,
> So near is God to man,
> When Duty whispers low, Thou must!
> The youth replies, I can!

> Or, if Virtue feeble were,
> Heaven itself would stoop to her.

II. Hymn.

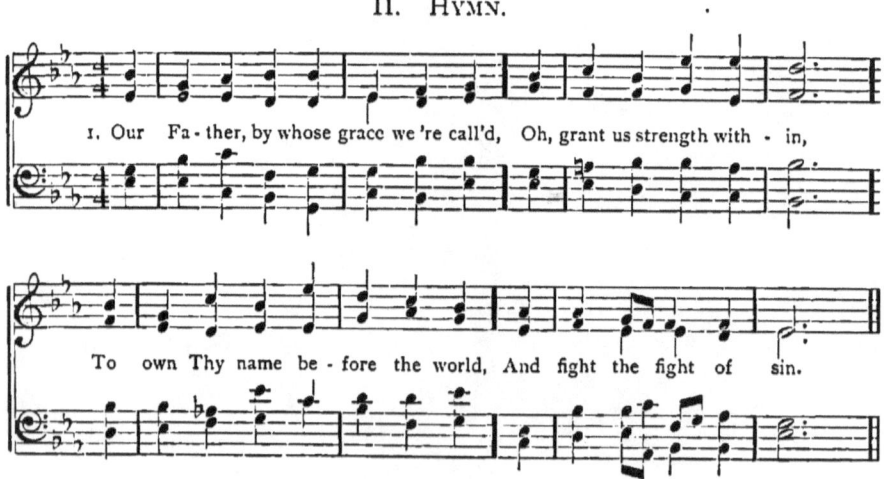

1. Our Father, by whose grace we're call'd, Oh, grant us strength within,
To own Thy name before the world, And fight the fight of sin.

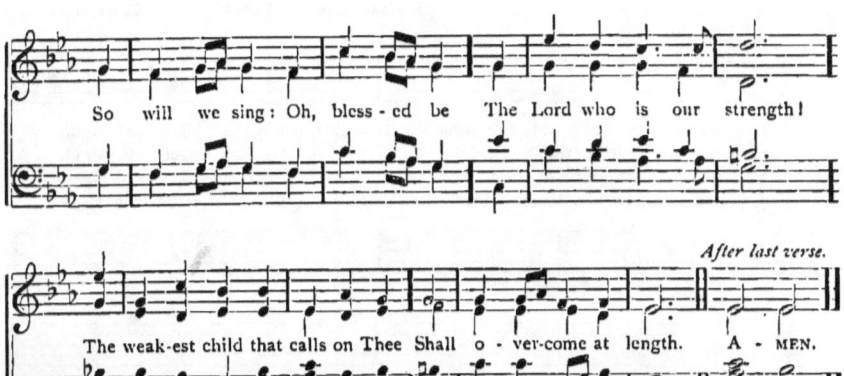

2 The swift may stumble in the race,
The strong in battle fall;
But they who ever seek Thy face
Shall in Thy might prevail.
So will we sing, etc.

3 And oh, when on each brow shall shine
Thy gift, a fadeless crown,
What joy to own the glory thine
And lowly cast it down!
So will we sing, etc.

III. Responsive Reading.

THEN said Jesus unto his disciples, If any man will come after me, let him deny himself, and take up his cross and follow me.

He that doth not take his cross and follow after me is not worthy of me.

In the world ye have tribulation; but be of good cheer, I have overcome the world.

He that endureth to the end shall be saved.

Take thy part in suffering hardship as a good soldier of Christ Jesus.

Walk worthily of the calling wherewith ye were called. Put on the whole armor of God.

Gird, therefore, your loins with truth. Put on the breastplate of righteousness. Take the shield of faith and the helmet of salvation and the sword of the spirit.

Fight the good fight of faith. Lay hold on eternal life.

Therefore, let us lay aside every weight, and the sin which doth so easily beset us, and let us run with patience the race that is set before us, looking unto Jesus, the author and perfecter of our faith, who, for the joy that was set before him, endured the cross, despising shame, and hath sat down at the right hand of the throne of God.

He that overcometh, I will give to him to sit down with me in my throne, as I also overcame, and sat down with my Father in His throne.

IV. Song. "Courage, Brother."

Words by Norman Macleod.   Music composed for this book by R. H. Clouston, Jr.

V. Prayer.

MOST merciful God, who art righteous in all Thy ways, and holy in all Thy works, and knowest our secret thoughts, help us, Thy children, to obey Thy voice and to serve Thee with all our souls. That we may not fall into sin, may we be watchful by night and by day. Make us more deeply grieved when we offend Thee, more glad to give Thee our whole hearts. As we grow in years, may we grow in wisdom and in favor with Thee, our God, and with men, our brethren. May we shun those who would lead us astray. Make our hearts clean in Thy sight. Help us to confess our faults and to lay aside our besetting sins. May we run with patience the race that is set before us. O thou Lover of Souls! grant Thy mighty help to us, Thy children, that we may do Thy blessed will and reach Thy house of many mansions. AMEN.

VI. Hymn.

Tenth Service.

THE TEACHINGS OF JESUS.

I. INTRODUCTORY SENTENCES.

ASK, and ye shall receive; seek, and ye shall find; knock, and it shall be opened unto you.

Blessed are they that hunger and thirst after righteousness; for they shall be filled.

Not every one that saith unto me, Lord, Lord, shall enter into the kingdom of heaven; but he that doeth the will of my Father who is in heaven.

II. EXHORTATION.

THE preparations of the heart are with God. Let us each inwardly pray that He will give us the spirit of Jesus, that our worship may be pleasing in His sight. We would be mindful how far off from God we should have been without this Sacred Teacher; and how near to the Father he will lead us, if we will humbly and steadfastly yield ourselves up to his guidance.

III. RESPONSES.

GLORY be to God! All glory be to Him who did, as on this day, create the light, and command it to shine on the face of the deep! How much more glorious is that light which shines in upon our minds by the revelations of prophets, the sweet solace of holy psalms, and by the heavenly teachings and blessed example of Jesus!

Blessed be the name of the Lord for this light which no darkness ever covers, this sun which never goes down.

That was the true light which lighteth every man that cometh into the world.

God is the Lord who hath given us such light.

IV. SONG. — BY THE SEA.

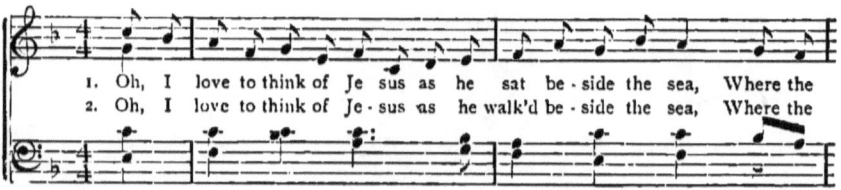

1. Oh, I love to think of Jesus as he sat be-side the sea, Where the
2. Oh, I love to think of Jesus as he walk'd be-side the sea, Where the

V. Responsive Reading.

THE spirit of the Lord is upon me, because He hath anointed me to preach good tidings to the poor. He hath sent me to heal the broken-hearted, to preach deliverance to the captives, and recovering of sight to the blind; to set at liberty them that are bound, to preach the acceptable year of the Lord.

Seek ye first the kingdom of God and His righteousness.

Lay not up for yourselves treasures upon the earth, where moth and rust doth consume, and where thieves break through and steal; but lay up for yourselves treasures in heaven, where neither moth nor rust doth consume, and where thieves do not break through and steal.

For where thy treasure is, there will thy heart be also.

Be not anxious for your life, what ye shall eat or what ye shall drink. Is not the life more than the food?

Come unto me, all ye that labor and are heavy laden, and I will give you rest.

Take my yoke upon you, and learn of me, for I am meek and lowly in heart; and ye shall find rest unto your souls:

For my yoke is easy, and my burden is light.

VI. Chant. — The Blessings of Jesus.

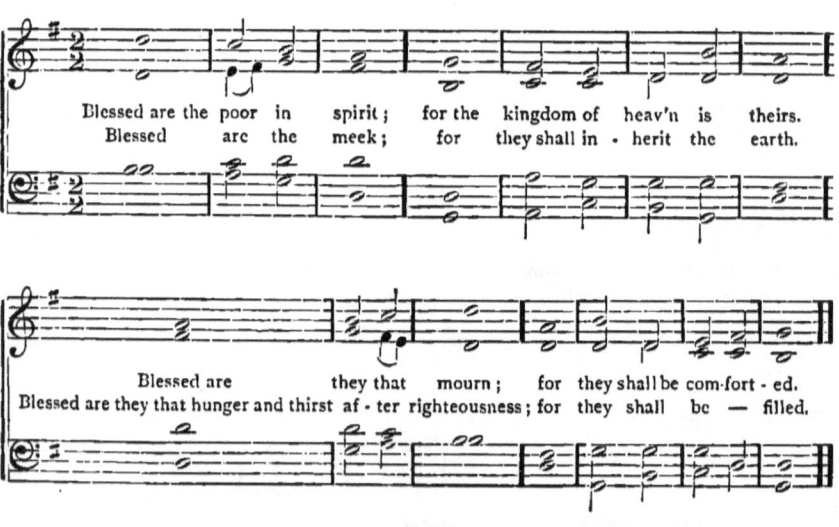

VII. Responsive Reading.

IF thy brother trespass against thee seven times in a day, forgive him; and if he trespass against thee seven times in a day, and seven times in a day turn again to thee, saying, I repent, — thou shalt forgive him. And I say not unto thee until seven times, but until seventy times seven.

Love your enemies; bless them that curse you; do good to them that hate you; and pray for them that despitefully use you and persecute you.

Take heed that ye do not your acts of righteousness before men, to be seen of them; otherwise ye have no reward of your Father who is in heaven.

Be ye therefore merciful, as your Father also is merciful.

Every good tree bringeth forth good fruit, but a corrupt tree bringeth forth evil fruit. Even so a good man, out of the good treasure of his heart, bringeth forth good things; and an evil man, out of the evil treasure of his heart, bringeth forth evil things.

Wherefore by their fruits shall ye know them.

Verily, I say unto you, Except ye be converted, and become as little children, ye shall not enter into the kingdom of heaven. But fear not; for it is your Father's good pleasure to give you the kingdom.

And I say unto you, There is joy in the presence of the angels of God over one sinner that repenteth.

All things, therefore, whatsoever ye would that men should do unto you, even so do ye also unto them.

This is my commandment, That ye love one another.

VIII. Chant. — The Blessings of Jesus.

Blessed are the mer-ci-ful; for they shall ob-tain — mercy.
Blessed are the peace-makers; for they shall be called the children of God

Blessed are the pure in heart; for they shall see — God.
Blessed are they that righteousness' sake; for the kingdom of heav'n is theirs. A-MEN.
are persecuted for

IX. Prayer.

O GOD, who didst send Thy word to speak in the prophets and live in Thy Son, we thank Thee for Jesus, who is the Way, the Truth, and the Life to our souls. We bless Thee that he came to seek and to save that which was lost; that he went about doing good; that he was the friend of the friendless; that he comforted the mourner, and bade the penitent depart in peace. We thank Thee for all the triumphs which attend his name. Especially do we praise Thee that we who have been born in a Christian land have such happy homes, such loving parents and kind friends, and that we enjoy so many and so great privileges of every kind.

May we now and always, O our Father, show forth our gratitude in lives devoted to Thy service. May that mild and affectionate spirit which Jesus breathed, flow into all our hearts, that we may help and bless our fellow-men, and make everybody around us happy. So shall we be true disciples, having within us the same heavenly mind which was in Jesus, and, like him, rejoicing always to do our Father's will. AMEN.

X. Hymn.

Eleventh Service.

LIFE ETERNAL.

I. Introductory Sentences.

BEHOLD, what manner of love the Father hath bestowed upon us, that we should be called the children of God!

Beloved, now are we children of God. And it doth not yet appear what we shall be; but we know that when it shall be made to appear, we shall be like Him, for we shall see Him as He is.

And every one that hath this hope in him purifieth himself, even as He is pure.

II. Hymn.

GERMAN.

1. Fa-ther, gra-cious Fa-ther! God of might and pow'r! Thou Thy-self art dwell-ing In us at this hour.
2. Yes! the hearts of chil-dren Hold what worlds can-not; And the God of won-ders Loves the low-ly spot.
3. Fa-ther, gra-cious Fa-ther! Thou art in us now; Fill us full of good-ness, Till our hearts o'er-flow.
4. Oh, how can we thank Thee For a gift like this,— Ev-en now that mak-eth Heav'n's e-ter-nal bliss? A-MEN.

III. Responsive Reading.

WE are not strangers or servants, but children of the household of God.
Thou wilt show me the path of life; in Thy presence is fulness of joy.
Man shall not live by bread alone, but by every word that proceedeth out of the mouth of God.
The kingdom of God is within you.
The Lord of heaven and earth dwelleth not in temples made with hands.
To be spiritually minded is life and peace.
The living Father sent me ; and I live because of the Father.
Lord, to whom shall we go? Thou hast the words of eternal life.
Be perfected, — live in peace ; and the God of love and peace shall be with you.
And let the beauty of the Lord our God be upon us.

IV. Gloria.

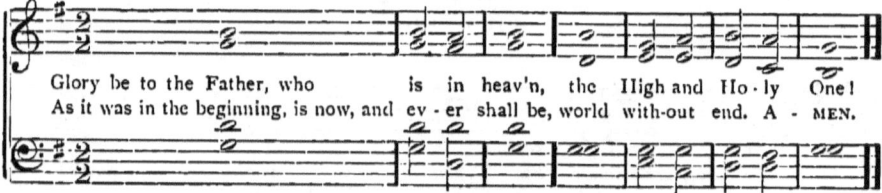

Glory be to the Father, who is in heav'n, the High and Ho-ly One!
As it was in the beginning, is now, and ev-er shall be, world with-out end. A - MEN.

V. Prayer.

O GOD, Fountain of all life, we thank Thee that we live and move and have our being in Thee. The world presses hard upon us, and we might faint and die if we were alone. But we are not alone, for the Father is with us. When the scenes of this world shall fade, Thy love will fold us to sleep ; and when we awake in the life to come, we shall be still with Thee, for in Thy love we shall live forever. Thou art from everlasting the same ; Thy years shall not fail. Our Father, help us to a deeper trust in the life everlasting, from the lesson of this one day. May we feel that this love which is now, ever shall be ; this work of life is the work Thou hast given us to do, and when it is done Thou wilt give us more : this love, that makes all our life so glad, flows out of the deep fountain of God, for God is love, and we shall love forever. Oh, set these lessons deep in our hearts ; help us day by day to see some rays of the eternal day that will break upon us at the last. May the gospel of Thy Son, the whisper of Thy Spirit, unite to make our faith in life eternal strong and clear. AMEN.

VI. Hymn.

Twelfth Service.

GOD OUR LIFE.

I. Introductory Sentences.

OH, magnify the Lord with me, and let us exalt His name together.
 Then ye shall call upon me, and go in peace; ye shall pray to me, and I will hear you; ye shall seek me, and find me, when ye search for me with all your heart.
 He that dwelleth in the secret place of the Most High, shall abide under the shadow of the Almighty.

II. Hymn.—"Though faint, yet pursuing."

Dr. Gauntlett.

Though faint, yet pur-su-ing, we go on our way; The Lord is our Leader, His word is our stay:

Though suff'ring and sorrow and tri-al be near, The Lord is our refuge, and whom can we fear?

III. Canticle.

MARVELLOUS things of the Lord our God have we heard, and our fathers have told us.

Repeat to their children His ancient praise, that the generations may set their hope in God.

They that trust in the Lord shall be as His holy hill, which cannot be removed;

As the mountains are round about Jerusalem, so the Lord encompasseth them forever.

ALL SING. [Music as before.]

> He raiseth the fallen, He cheereth the faint;
> The weak and oppress'd, He will hear their complaint.
> The way may be weary, and thorny the road;
> But how can we falter? — our help is in God!

IV. Canticle.

THE secret of the Lord is with them that fear Him: in the time of trouble He hideth them in His pavilion.

In the day-time He leadeth them with a cloud, and in the night with a light of fire.

Though they fall, they shall not be utterly cast down, for the Lord upholdeth them with His arm.

Commit thy way unto the Lord; wait patiently for Him, and thou shalt never be forsaken.

He will draw thee out of the dark waters, and show thee the path of life.

ALL SING. [Music as before.]

> Though clouds may surround us, our God is our light;
> Though storms rage around us, our God is our might:
> So faint, yet pursuing, still onward we go;
> The Lord is our Leader, no fear can we know.

A - MEN.

V. Prayer.

OUR Heavenly Father, we praise Thee as the giver of all our blessings. Day by day may our grateful hearts turn unto Thee; and may we become ever more and more faithful in Thy service. Thou hast been good and true unto us: may we be good and true to one another. We would feel that we can best make return for Thy love by loving Thee and those of Thy children with whom Thou hast placed our lives. We would love our parents and teachers, our friends and companions, — all to whom we can do good. May we be assured that with Thee and in Thy love we shall always be safe. Thou art helping us through each day, and watching over us every night. May we feel that through all our day of life Thou wilt bless our souls; and that when the night of death shall come upon us, Thou wilt lead us through the darkness unto the eternal glory. Praise be unto Thee for all Thy goodness, forever and ever. AMEN.

VI. Hymn.

Thirteenth Service.

WHO FORGIVETH ALL THY SINS.

I. Hymn.

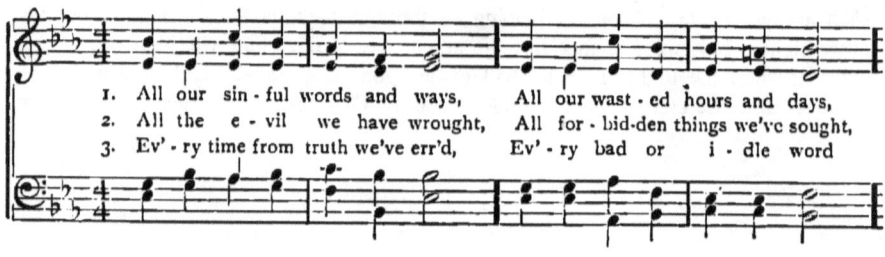

1. All our sin-ful words and ways, All our wast-ed hours and days,
2. All the e-vil we have wrought, All for-bid-den things we've sought,
3. Ev'-ry time from truth we've err'd, Ev'-ry bad or i-dle word

After last verse.

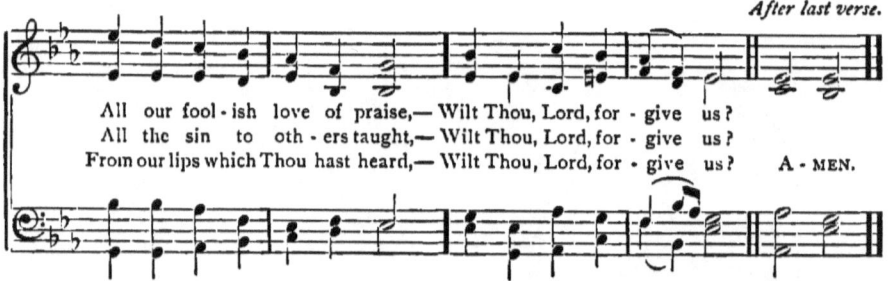

All our fool-ish love of praise,— Wilt Thou, Lord, for-give us?
All the sin to oth-ers taught,— Wilt Thou, Lord, for-give us?
From our lips which Thou hast heard,— Wilt Thou, Lord, for-give us? A-MEN.

 4 All the help we need each day
  That we may not fall away,
  Or from Thee e'er go astray,—
   Grant us, Heav'nly Father!

 5 Faith to see Thee ever near,
  Hope to check each foolish fear,
  Constant strength to persevere,—
   Grant us, Heav'nly Father!

   6 Ev'ry needful gift of grace,
    Till we reach the holy place,
    Where we shall behold Thy face,—
     Grant us, Heav'nly Father! AMEN.

II. Responsive Reading.

I SAID I will confess my transgressions unto the Lord; and Thou forgavest the iniquity of my sin.

Whoso confesseth and forsaketh his sins shall have mercy.

If we say that we have no sin, we deceive ourselves, and the truth is not in us.

If we confess our sins, God is faithful and just to forgive us our sins.

Let the wicked forsake his way, and the unrighteous man his thoughts; and let him return unto the Lord, and He will have mercy upon him.

The Lord is gracious and full of compassion, slow to anger, and of great mercy.

With everlasting remembrance will I have mercy upon thee, saith the Lord, thy Redeemer.

He restoreth my soul; He leadeth me in the paths of righteousness, for His name's sake.

III. Chant.

Praise the Lord, O my soul; and all that is within me praise His ho-ly Name.
Who forgiveth all thy sins, and healeth all thine in-fir-mi-ties;
Glory be to the Father, who is in heav'n, the High and Ho-ly One;

Praise the Lord, O my soul, and forget not all His ben-e-fits;
Who saveth thy life from de-struction, { and crowneth thee with mercy and } lov-ing kind-ness.
As it was in the beginning, is now, and ev-er shall be, world with-out end. A-MEN.

IV. Scripture Reading by Superintendent.

[Luke xv. 11-32; or, Matt. xviii. 21-35.]

V. Prayer.

O GOD most holy, who art a gracious and a tender Father to those who turn unto Thee, look upon us in Thy great love. Show us our sins as they truly are. We are heartily sorry for them. Help us to forsake them. Pardon us for every act of wrong-doing, for every evil passion, every unkind feeling, every sinful wish. May we watch and pray that we enter no more into temptation; and wilt Thou, O God, deliver us from all evil. Search us, O Lord, and know our hearts; try us, and know our thoughts, and see if there be any wicked way in us; and lead us in the way everlasting. AMEN.

VI. Hymn.

Fourteenth Service.

FOLLOWING AFTER THE SPIRIT OF JESUS.

I. Introductory Sentences.

THE dayspring from on high hath visited us, to give light to them that sit in darkness and in the shadow of death, to guide our feet into the way of peace.

God, who commanded the light to shine out of darkness, hath shined in our hearts, to give the light of the knowledge of the glory of God, in the face of Jesus Christ.

God hath sent forth the spirit of His Son into our hearts, crying, Abba, Father!

II. Hymn. — The Sacred Teacher.

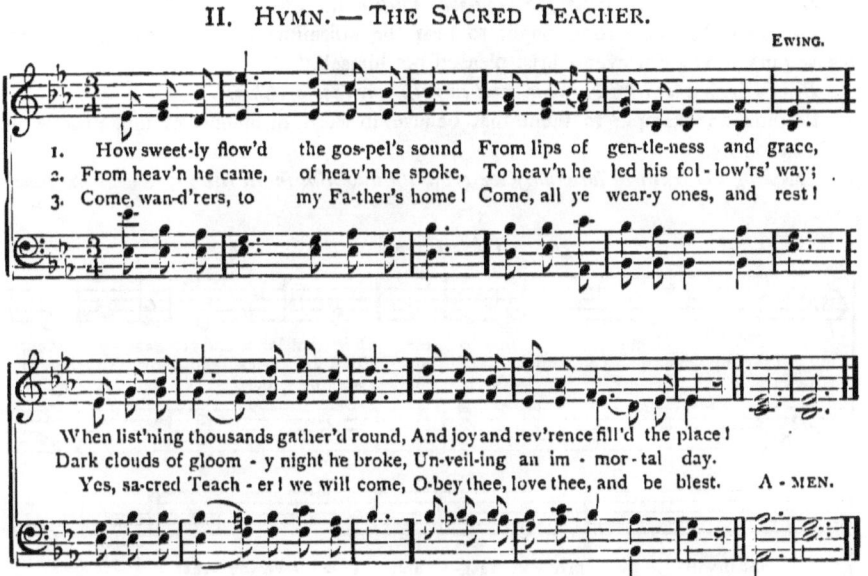

EWING.

1. How sweet-ly flow'd the gos-pel's sound From lips of gen-tle-ness and grace,
2. From heav'n he came, of heav'n he spoke, To heav'n he led his fol-low'rs' way;
3. Come, wan-d'rers, to my Fa-ther's home! Come, all ye wear-y ones, and rest!

When list'ning thousands gather'd round, And joy and rev'rence fill'd the place!
Dark clouds of gloom-y night he broke, Un-veil-ing an im-mor-tal day.
Yes, sa-cred Teach-er! we will come, O-bey thee, love thee, and be blest. A-MEN.

III. RESPONSIVE READING.

AND the child Jesus grew, and waxed strong in spirit, filled with wisdom; and the grace of God was upon him.

He went down with his parents, and was subject unto them; and increased in wisdom, and stature, and in favor with God and man.

Though he were a Son, yet learned he obedience by the things which he suffered.

Christ suffered for us, leaving us an example that we should follow his steps.

For it became Him for whom are all things, and by whom are all things, in bringing many sons unto glory, to make the Captain of their salvation perfect through sufferings.

If any man will come after me, let him deny himself, and take up his cross, and follow me.

To this end was I born, and for this cause came I into the world, that I should bear witness unto the truth.

I must work the works of Him that sent me, while it is day.

The Son of man came not to be ministered unto, but to minister.

He went about doing good, for God was with him.

We, then, that are strong, ought to bear the infirmities of the weak, and not to please ourselves. For even Christ pleased not himself.

Bear ye one another's burdens, and so fulfil the law of Christ.

Be thou an example to them that believe, in word, in manner of life, in love, in faith, in purity.

Speaking the truth in love, may we grow up into him in all things, who is the head.

IV. CHANT.

V. Prayer.

LORD of all power and might, who art the author and giver of all good things, we would feel that Thou art near us now, and that we ever live in Thee. Thou speakest to our hearts. May we obey Thy voice. By Thy good Spirit, Thou leadest us in the way we should go. May we ever follow Thee. Here may we learn the things Thou wouldst have us to do, and grow strong to do them. We bless Thee for the precepts and the life of Jesus, who has set us the example of what we should strive to be. May we walk in the light which shines from him; and every day may we live the life that never dies. Amen.

VI. Hymn.

Fifteenth Service.

THE BLESSED LIFE.

I. Introductory Sentences.

BLESSED is the man that feareth the Lord, that delighteth greatly in His commandments.

Blessed is the man that walketh not in the counsel of the ungodly, nor standeth in the way of sinners; but his delight is in the law of the Lord, and in His law doth he meditate day and night.

Seek first the kingdom of God and His righteousness, and all these things shall be added unto you.

II. Hymn. — The Greatest Blessing.

GERMAN MELODY.

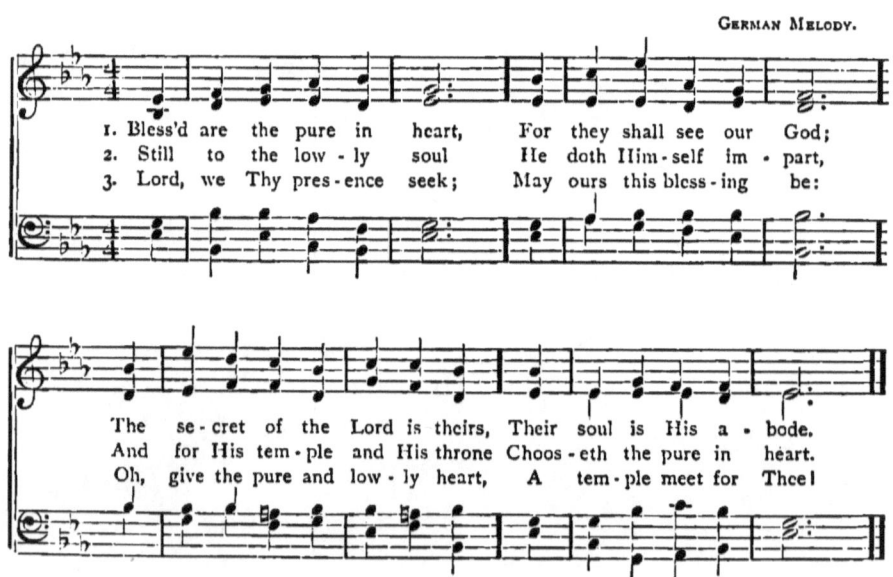

1. Bless'd are the pure in heart, For they shall see our God;
   The se-cret of the Lord is theirs, Their soul is His a-bode.
2. Still to the low-ly soul He doth Him-self im-part,
   And for His tem-ple and His throne Choos-eth the pure in heart.
3. Lord, we Thy pres-ence seek; May ours this bless-ing be:
   Oh, give the pure and low-ly heart, A tem-ple meet for Thee!

III. Responsive Reading.

AND seeing the multitudes, Jesus went up into the mountain: and when he had sat down, his disciples came unto him: and he opened his mouth and taught them, saying:

Blessed are the poor in spirit; for theirs is the kingdom of heaven.

The Lord is nigh unto them that are of a broken heart, and saveth such as be of a contrite spirit.

Blessed are they that mourn; for they shall be comforted.

Happy is the man whom God correcteth; for He woundeth, and His hands make whole.

Blessed are the meek; for they shall inherit the earth.

The meek will He guide in judgment, and the meek will He teach His way.

Blessed are they that hunger and thirst after righteousness; for they shall be filled.

He shall receive the blessing from the Lord, and righteousness from the God of his salvation.

Blessed are the merciful; for they shall obtain mercy.

Blessed is he that considereth the poor: the Lord will deliver him in time of trouble.

Blessed are the pure in heart; for they shall see God.

Blessed are the undefiled in the way, who walk in the law of the Lord.

Blessed are the peace-makers; for they shall be called the children of God.

Behold how good and how pleasant it is for brethren to dwell together in unity!

Blessed are they that are persecuted for righteousness' sake; for theirs is the kingdom of heaven.

For Thou, Lord, wilt bless the righteous; with favor wilt Thou compass him, as with a shield.

Blessed are ye when men shall revile you and persecute you, and shall say all manner of evil against you falsely, for my sake.

Unto the upright there ariseth light in the darkness: the righteous shall be in everlasting remembrance.

Rejoice and be exceeding glad; for great is your reward in heaven: for so persecuted they the prophets who were before you.

All these blessings shall come upon thee, if thou shalt hearken unto the voice of the Lord thy God.

The Lord shall preserve thy going out and thy coming in, from this time forth and even for evermore.

IV. Gloria in Excelsis.

E. J. Hopkins.

V. Prayer.

O THOU who art Love, may we dwell in love, that we may dwell in Thee. May we obey Thy commandments. Incline our hearts to keep Thy laws. Give us, O Lord, the wisdom which is from above; which is first pure, then peaceable, full of mercy and good fruits. May we love our neighbor as ourselves. May we be kind to one another, tender-hearted, forgiving one another. May the law of the spirit of life in Christ Jesus make us free from the law of sin; and may we always follow after the things which make for peace. So may we let our light shine before men that they may see our good works, and give the glory, not unto us, but unto Thee, to whom all praise belongs. AMEN.

VI. Hymn.

Sixteenth Service.

GOD EVER PRESENT.

I. Hymn.

II. Introductory Sentences.

THERE is one living and true God, the Maker and Preserver of all things.
Nothing is hidden from God's sight. The Divine Reason presides over the universe, and fills all parts of it.
We can do nothing without the help of God, and that from moment to moment.

III. Prayer.

O GOD, Thou art our hope; on Thee alone do we rest. Thou carest for every one of us as if Thou didst care only for him; and Thou carest for all as if all were but one. Thou art ever with us; we need not go anywhere to find Thee, for Thou art nearer to us than we are to ourselves. Can we know Thee, O God, and not love Thee? Can we remember that Thou seest us, and forget to do the things which please Thee? Cleanse us from all our secret faults. Keep us back from every open sin. May all that we say and all that we do be acceptable in Thy sight, O Lord, our Strength and our Redeemer. AMEN.

IV. Hymn.

V. Responsive Reading.

O LORD, Thou hast searched me and known me!
Thou knowest my sitting down and my rising up;
Thou understandest my thoughts from afar;
Thou seest my path and my lying down;
Thou art acquainted with all my ways.

For before the word is upon my tongue,
Behold, O Lord, Thou knowest it altogether!
> *Thou besettest me behind and before,*
> *And layest Thy hand upon me.*

Such knowledge is too wonderful for me;
> *It is high, I cannot attain to it.*

Whither shall I go from Thy Spirit?
> *Whither shall I flee from Thy presence?*

If I ascend up into heaven, Thou art there!
> *If I make my bed in the underworld, behold, Thou art there!*

If I take the wings of the morning,
And dwell in the uttermost parts of the sea,
Even there shall Thy hand lead me;
> *Thy right hand shall hold me!*

If I say, "Surely the darkness shall cover me!"
Even the night shall be light about me:
> *Yea, the darkness hideth not from Thee,*
> *But the night shineth as the day.*

The darkness and the light are both alike to Thee.
> *For Thou knowest what is in the darkness,*
> *And the light dwelleth with Thee.*

VI. HYMN.

Seventeenth Service.

WORSHIP.

I. Hymn.

II. Introductory Sentences.

ALL that is in the heavens and the earth praiseth God; and He is the Mighty, the Wise.

Moses cried, O Lord, where shall I find Thee? And God said, When thou seekest Me, thou hast already found Me.

God's pleasure is in the piety and devotion of consecrated hearts; and to love and serve all men is to delight in God.

III. Prayer.

O THOU whom we worship, our God and our Father, to Thee we turn for light and love and blessing. Gathered in this dear place, we seek to remember those truths that give our souls true life. Help us to break the fetters of evil. Lead our feet in the beautiful paths of virtue. Guard our thoughts from temptation; make us strong in goodness. Because of Thy mercy we would sing Thy praise with our whole hearts. May Thy kingdom come unto us and unto all. We ask these things as Thy children. Amen.

IV. Hymn.

V. Responsive Reading.

MAKE a joyful noise unto God, O all ye lands!
  Sing forth the honor of His name!
All the earth shall worship Thee;
  Thou rulest by Thy power forever.
Oh, praise our God, ye people!
  Who holdeth our soul in life.
I will go into Thy house with offerings:
  I will pay Thee my vows.
Oh, give thanks unto the Lord, for He is good!
  For His mercy endureth forever.
Worship the Lord in the beauty of holiness!
  Give unto the Lord the glory due unto His name.
Send out Thy light and Thy truth!
  Let them lead me.

VI. Hymn.

Closing Services.

[THESE SERVICES MAY BE USED FOR ANY SUNDAY.]

FIRST SERVICE.

This may begin with

A Hymn.

Then may be said

The Prayers.

GRANT, we beseech Thee, our Heavenly Father, that the words we have heard this day may, through Thy Spirit, be so grafted in our hearts that they shall bring forth in us the fruit of good living, to the honor of Thy holy name. Trustful and grateful, we give ourselves to Thy keeping and Thy guidance; and would pray, as Thy beloved Son has taught us, —

Our Father, who art in heaven: Hallowed be Thy name. Thy kingdom come. Thy will be done on earth, as it is in heaven. Give us this day our daily bread. And forgive us our trespasses, as we forgive those who trespass against us. And lead us not into temptation; but deliver us from evil. For Thine is the kingdom, and the power, and the glory, forever and ever. AMEN.

Then may be added

The Benediction and Response.

THE Lord preserve our going out and our coming in, from this time forth and even for evermore.

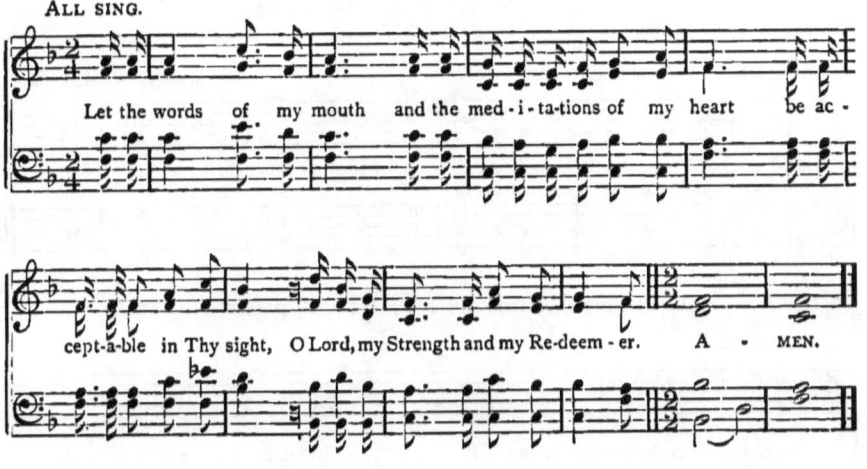

SECOND SERVICE.

This may begin with

A Hymn.

Then may be said

The Prayers.

LORD of all power and might, who art the Author and Giver of all good things, graft in our hearts the love of Thy name; increase in us true religion; nourish us with all goodness. Grant us in this world knowledge of Thy truth; and in the world to come, life everlasting. AMEN.

Our Father, who art in heaven: Hallowed by Thy name. Thy kingdom come. Thy will be done on earth, as it is in heaven. Give us this day our daily bread. And forgive us our trespasses, as we forgive those who trespass against us. And lead us not into temptation; but deliver us from evil. For Thine is the kingdom, and the power, and the glory, for ever and ever. AMEN.

Then may follow

The Benediction and Response.

THE Lord is thy keeper: behold, He that keepeth thee shall neither slumber nor sleep.

ALL SING.   Music by W. H. Lyon.

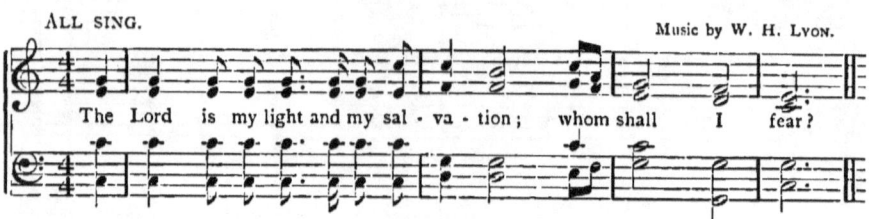

The Lord is my light and my sal-va-tion; whom shall I fear?

The Lord shall preserve thee from all evil; He shall preserve thy soul.

ALL SING.

The Lord is the strength of my life; of whom shall I be a-fraid?

The Lord shall preserve thy going out and thy coming in, from this time forth and even for evermore.

A - MEN.

THIRD SERVICE.

This may begin with

A HYMN.

Then may be said

THE PRAYERS.

OUR Heavenly Father, keep us, we beseech Thee, under the protection of Thy good providence, and make us to have continually a love of Thy holy name. Wherever we are, may we remember that Thou, O God, seest us. Be near at all times to direct, sanctify, and preserve. Let not evil communications corrupt our minds, nor sinful desires prevail against our souls; but may we always hear Thy voice, obey Thy word, and live to Thy glory. We ask it as disciples of Jesus; and we would pray as he has taught us, —

Our Father, who art in heaven: Hallowed be Thy name. Thy kingdom come. Thy will be done on earth, as it is in heaven. Give us this day our daily bread. And forgive us our trespasses, as we forgive those who trespass against us. And lead us not into temptation; but deliver us from evil. For Thine is the kingdom, and the power, and the glory, for ever and ever. AMEN.

THE CLOSING ANTHEM.

Let the peo-ple praise Thee, O God; yea, let all the peo-ple praise Thee. Let the na-tions re-joice, re-joice and give thanks, re-joice and give thanks, re-joice and give thanks.

DOXOLOGY.

1. For mer-cies past we praise Thee, Lord,— The fruits of earth, the hopes of heav'n, Thy help-ing arm, Thy guid-ing word, And an-swer'd prav'rs, and sins for-giv'n.
2. When-e'er we tread on dan-ger's height, Or walk temp-ta-tion's slip-p'ry way, Be still, to lead our steps a-right, Thy word our guide, Thine arm our stay.

Then may be added

THE BENEDICTION.

THE Lord bless us and keep us. The Lord make His face to shine upon us, and be gracious unto us. The Lord lift up the light of His countenance upon us, and give us peace.

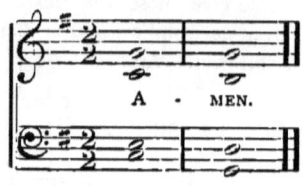

FOURTH SERVICE.

The Service may begin with

A HYMN.

Then may be said

THE PRAYERS.

WE ask Thy blessing, O Father, for this day, and for all the days that are before us. Help us that in keeping Thy commandments we may please Thee both in will and deed. Give us, we pray Thee, daily strength for daily needs. Come to us often in holy thoughts and reverent feelings, and thus deliver us from evil. May all that is beautiful remind us of Thee, the Infinite Beauty. May all that is true lead us to Thee, the source of all truth. In the faith of Thy dear Son, may we love and serve Thee unto our life's end. AMEN.

OUR FATHER, who art in heaven : Hallowed be Thy name. Thy kingdom come. Thy will be done on earth, as it is in heaven. Give us this day our daily bread. And forgive us our trespasses, as we forgive those who trespass against us. And lead us not into temptation ; but deliver us from evil. For Thine is the kingdom, and the power, and the glory, for ever and ever. AMEN.

Then may be added

THE BENEDICTIONS.

NOW may the peace of God rule in our hearts; and the word of Christ dwell in us richly in all wisdom.

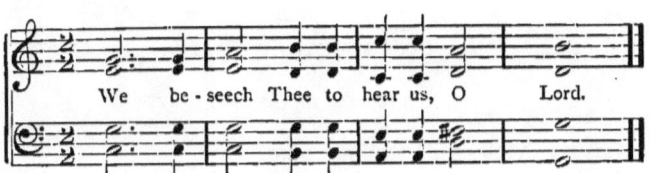

May our hearts repeat the song of the angels: " Glory to God in the highest; on earth peace, good-will to men!"

ALL SING. [Music as before.]

May the kingdom of God come in all the earth; and may His will be done here as it is in heaven.

First Special Service.

ANNIVERSARY.

I. Introductory Psalm.

To be said in Concert.

THE Lord is my shepherd; I shall not want.

He maketh me to lie down in green pastures; He leadeth me beside the still waters.

He restoreth my soul; He leadeth me in the paths of righteousness for His name's sake.

Yea, though I walk through the valley of the shadow of death, I will fear no evil; for Thou art with me; Thy rod and Thy staff they comfort me.

Thou preparest a table before me in the presence of my enemies; Thou anointest my head with oil; my cup runneth over.

Surely, goodness and mercy shall follow me all the days of my life; and I will dwell in the house of the Lord forever.

II. A Psalm of Praise.

MAKE a joyful noise unto the Lord, all the earth.

ALL SING.

Hal - le - lu - jah! hal - le - lu - jah! hal - le - lu - jah! A - - men.

Serve the Lord with gladness; come before His presence with singing. Hallelujah! etc.

Know ye that the Lord He is God: it is He that hath made us, and not we ourselves; we are His people, and the sheep of His pasture.

Hallelujah! etc.

Enter into His gates with thanksgiving, and into His courts with praise; be thankful unto Him, and bless His name.

Hallelujah! etc.

For the Lord is good; His mercy is everlasting, and His truth endureth to all generations.

Hallelujah! etc.

III. Responsive Canticle.

I WAS glad when my companions said unto me, Come, it is our holy day;
Let us go into the house of the Lord: let us take sweet counsel together;
Let our feet stand within His gates, and heart and voice give thanks unto Him.
Blessed be the temple hallowed by His name: pray for peace within its walls:
Peace to young and old that enter there, peace to every soul abiding therein.
For friends' and brethren's sake, I will never cease to say, Peace be within thee!
What though for Him who filleth heaven and earth, there can be no dwelling made with hands;
What though His way is in the deep, and His knowledge too wonderful for us, and before Him we are as children that cannot speak:
Yet, touched by the altar's living glow, we learn, as an infant, to lisp His name;
And try the wings that beat for His refuge, and flee as a bird to the mountain.
O Lord, when we cry unto Thee from the deep, and wait for Thee as they that wait for the morning,
Thou wilt have regard to our entreaty: the sigh of the lowly Thou wilt not despise.
Not long, O Lord, shall we feel after Thee in these courts below; not long wilt Thou hearken to these faltering lips.
Our fathers Thou hast called to Thy higher praise; and gathered to their fathers must all the children be.
Let the dead and living praise thee, O God, above, below; let all the generations praise thee.
Let the glorified company of the first-born, whose names are in the Book of Life:
Let angels in the height praise Thee, who dwellest in the heavens;
Let Thy Church on earth praise Thee, the delight of whose Wisdom is in the children of men.
O House of the Lord's praise, peace be to them that love thee!

IV. Gloria.

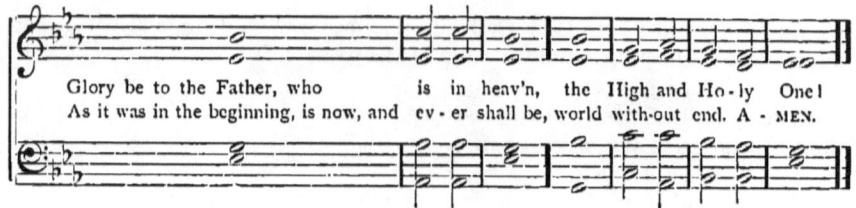

Glory be to the Father, who is in heav'n, the High and Ho-ly One!
As it was in the beginning, is now, and ev-er shall be, world with-out end. A-men.

V. Prayer.

MOST merciful Father, Thou hast made the heavens fair above our heads and the earth beautiful beneath our feet. Thou givest health to our bodies, and fillest our hearts with joy. We thank Thee for the year that is past; for the support of every minute, and the gifts of every day; for all the good we may have done, the sins we have resisted, the temptations we have overcome. We thank Thee for loving parents, wise teachers, and kind friends, and for all who have helped us to lead the good life. We thank Thee for the blessed words and heavenly example of Jesus, for the helps of Thy spirit, and the promises of the Gospel. We bless Thee for the memory of the righteous, and especially for those who were dear to us, who lived in faith and departed in peace. To-day, as we think of all Thy goodness and Thy great loving-kindness, may we resolve to do more for Thee in the year that is before us. Obeying Thy commandments, keeping our hearts from evil, and doing good as we have opportunity, may we walk always according to Thy holy will; so that even while here below, heaven shall be opening to us its bliss and its glory. Amen.

VI. Anniversary Hymn.

1. In this hal-low'd dwell - ing, House of pray'r and praise,
2. All things tell His glo - ry,— Earth and heav'n a - bove;
3. Then, with-in this dwell - ing, Raise the joy - ful song;

Second Special Service.

IN MEMORIAM.

I. Introductory Verses.

WHAT is excellent,
  As God lives, is permanent.
Hearts are dust; hearts' loves remain.
Hearts' love will meet thee again.

Thither our weak and weary steps are tending;
  O loving Father, still with us abide!
Guide us toward home, where, all our wanderings ending,
  We then shall see Thee, and be satisfied.

II. Hymn.

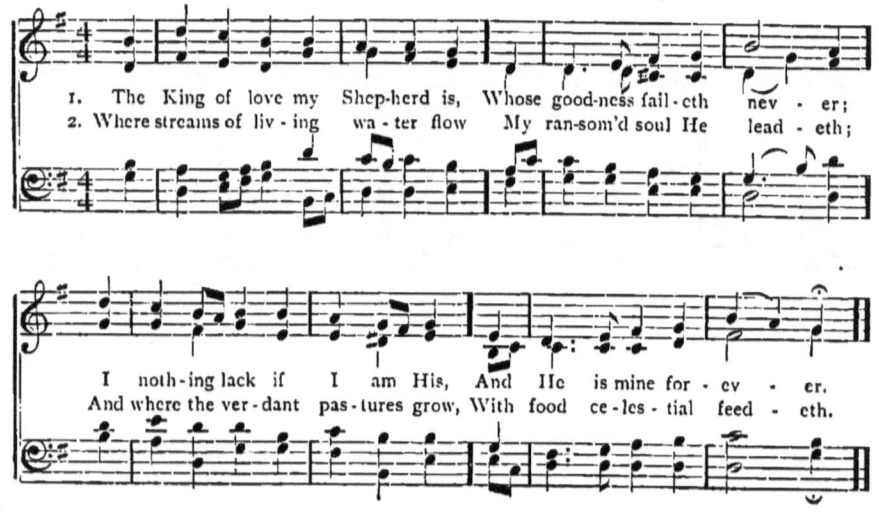

1. The King of love my Shepherd is, Whose goodness faileth never;
   I nothing lack if I am His, And He is mine forever.
2. Where streams of living water flow My ransom'd soul He leadeth;
   And where the verdant pastures grow, With food celestial feedeth.

III. Responsive Reading.

THE eternal God is thy refuge; and underneath are the everlasting arms.
Thou shalt guide me by Thy counsel, and afterward receive me to glory.
Yea, though I walk through the valley of the shadow of death, I will fear no evil:
For Thou art with me; Thy rod and Thy staff they comfort me.
For we know that if our earthly house of this tabernacle were dissolved, we have a building of God, a house not made with hands, eternal in the heavens.
And there shall be no night there.
They shall hunger no more, neither thirst any more; neither shall the sun light on them, nor any heat.
And they need no candle, neither light of the sun; for the Lord God giveth them light.
And there shall be no more death, neither sorrow nor crying; neither shall there be any more pain.
For the former things are passed away.
The things which are seen are temporal.
But the things which are not seen are eternal.

IV. Hymn.

3. In death's dark vale I fear no ill, With Thee, dear Lord, beside me;
Thy rod and staff my comfort still, Thy hand of love to guide me.
4. And so, through all the length of days, Thy goodness faileth never;
Good Shepherd, may I sing Thy praise Within Thy house forever! A-MEN.

V. Reading by Superintendent.

[Matt. xix. 13-15, and xviii. 1-5, and verse 10; or, Rev. xiv. 13, and xxi. 1-4.]

VI. Prayer.

O GOD of love, in Thy hand is our life. Thou doest all things well. In love Thou didst create us; in love Thou dost preserve us; and in equal love Thou appointest for each one of us the day of his death. In Thy mercy Thou hast taken one who was dear to us; may we say from our hearts, Thy will be done! We thank Thee for the sweet memory of blessings which are for a time withdrawn from us, and for the immortal hope which no earthly loss can ever darken. Comfort us with holy thoughts of our heavenly home. Knowing that Thou art God, may our complaining cease. Give to each one of us the gracious spirit of Thy Son, that amid all the changes of life we may be Thy loving and obedient children. Keep us from falling, and at length present us blameless in the presence of Thy glory, with exceeding joy.

So pray we, as followers of Jesus. AMEN.

VII. Chant.

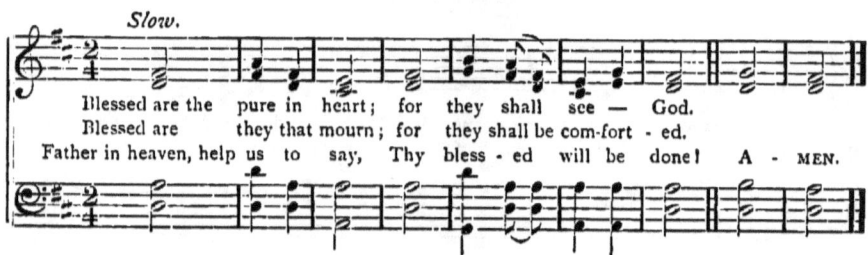

Blessed are the pure in heart; for they shall see — God.
Blessed are they that mourn; for they shall be com-fort-ed.
Father in heaven, help us to say, Thy bless-ed will be done! A-MEN.

Third Special Service.

NATIONAL.

I. Introductory Sentences.

WE have heard with our ears, O God, our fathers have told us, what work Thou didst in their days, in the times of old.

For they got not the land in possession by their own sword, neither did their own arm save them; but Thy right hand and Thine arm, and the light of Thy countenance, because Thou hadst a favor unto them.

When our fathers were but few in number, yea, very few, and strangers in the land; when they went from one nation to another, from one kingdom to another people,— He suffered no man to do them wrong; yea, He reproved kings for their sakes.

II. Metrical Chant,— Remembrance of our Fathers.

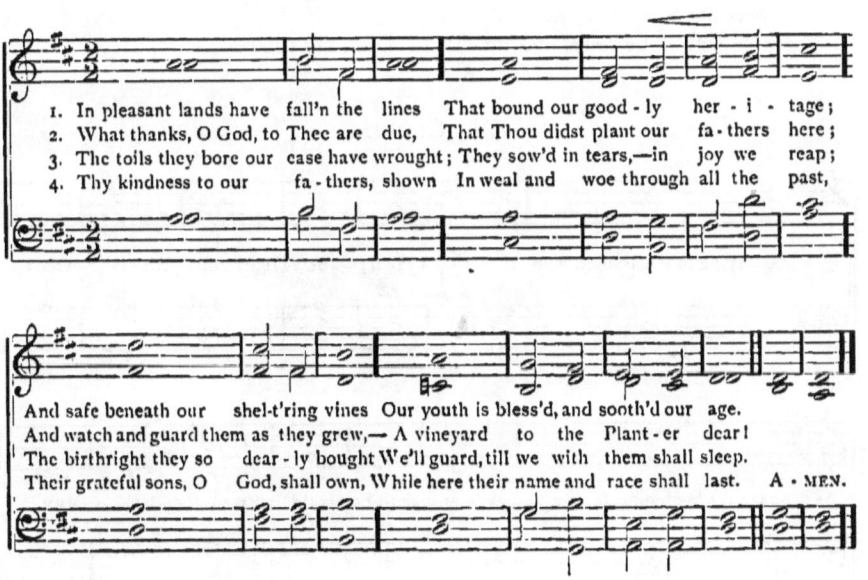

1. In pleasant lands have fall'n the lines That bound our good-ly her-i-tage; And safe beneath our shel-t'ring vines Our youth is bless'd, and sooth'd our age.
2. What thanks, O God, to Thee are due, That Thou didst plant our fa-thers here; And watch and guard them as they grew,— A vineyard to the Plant-er dear!
3. The toils they bore our ease have wrought; They sow'd in tears,—in joy we reap; The birthright they so dear-ly bought We'll guard, till we with them shall sleep.
4. Thy kindness to our fa-thers, shown In weal and woe through all the past, Their grateful sons, O God, shall own, While here their name and race shall last. A-MEN.

III. Responsive Readings.

COME near, ye nations, to hear; and hearken, ye people: let the earth hear, and all that is therein; the world, and all things that come forth of it.

For the Lord is our Judge, the Lord is our Lawgiver, the Lord is our King, — He will save us.

I will exalt Thee, O God, I will praise Thy name; for Thou hast done wonderful things.

Thy counsels of old are faithfulness and truth.

Our fathers trusted in Thee, O Lord;

They trusted, and Thou didst deliver them.

They cried unto Thee, and were delivered;

They trusted in Thee, and were not confounded.

Righteousness exalteth a nation;

But sin is a reproach to any people.

When the righteous are in authority, the people rejoice;

But when the wicked bear rule, the people mourn.

Oh, Lord God of our fathers, art not Thou God in heaven?

The God of heaven, He will prosper us.

Execute the judgment of truth and peace in your gates.

Love the truth and peace.

Peace be within thy walls, and prosperity within thy palaces.

IV. Gloria.

Glory be to the Father, who is in heav'n; the High and Holy One:

As it was in the beginning, is now, and ever shall be, world without end. A - MEN.

V. Prayer.

LORD of every heart, and Ruler of all nations, we thank Thee for Thy goodness and loving-kindness to us and to all men. We bless Thee for our country, under whose shelter and defence our homes, our schools, and our churches are preserved. We thank Thee for our fathers, who rose in arms and struck off the chains that bound them, and made this nation free. And we bless Thee for the brave men who in later times, when slavery threatened the nation's life, went forth from happy homes and peaceful toils into the rude tumult of war; who dared all, and gave all, even their own lives, that liberty and the land of liberty might be saved. By the voices of all Thy heroes who died for truth, for freedom, and for their country, Thou givest us the assurance that Thou wilt freely bestow all things upon those who are led by the same spirit. May we follow their example, and become useful citizens. May we always be ready to do our part to promote the public good, and to make our country and the world better for our having lived therein. May the glorious gospel of the Prince of Peace more widely prevail; that truth and justice, purity and temperance, religion and piety, may be established among us for all generations. So may the law of Christ be fulfilled, and the heavenly kingdom come upon earth. AMEN.

VI. Hymn.

Fourth Special Service.

HARVEST.

I. Hymn of Praise.

II. Introductory Sentences.

OH, magnify the Lord with me, and let us exalt His name together!
It is a good thing to give thanks unto the Lord, and to sing praises unto Thy name, O Thou Most High.

For Thou, Lord, hast made me glad through Thy works; and I will rejoice in giving praise for the operations of Thy hands.

III. Gloria.

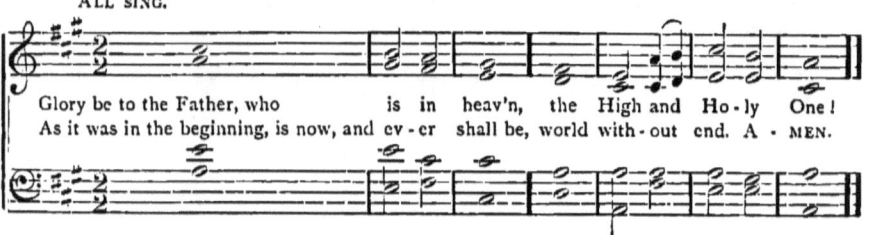

ALL SING.

Glory be to the Father, who is in heav'n, the High and Ho-ly One!
As it was in the beginning, is now, and ev-er shall be, world with-out end. A-MEN.

IV. Exhortation.

ASSEMBLED here to render thanks for the great benefits we have received at God's hands, and to set forth His most worthy praise, let us beseech Him to grant us the grace of a humble and holy spirit; that the thanksgivings which we offer up with one voice and one heart may be acceptable unto Him, our Maker, our Strength, and our Redeemer.

V. Prayer.

WE bless Thee, O God, for Thy goodness which crowns each passing year; for Thy tender mercies which are over all Thy works. Once more has harvest followed seed-time, and the earth again yields us her increase. Thou openest unto us Thy good treasure; Thou commandest the blessing upon us in our storehouses; Thou makest us plenteous in the fruits of the ground. For all these bounties of Thy hand we praise Thee, beseeching Thee to continue to us Thy loving-kindness in the years that are to come. May we glorify Thee by bearing in our lives the rich fruits of the Spirit: precious harvests of love and good-will, long-suffering and gentleness, faith and meekness, with every grace and every virtue of the Christian character. And may we never weary in well-doing, so that in due time we may reap the promised reward. AMEN.

VI. Responsive Reading.

THE heavens declare the glory of God; and the firmament showeth His handiwork.

Day unto day uttereth speech, and night unto night showeth knowledge.

The day is Thine, O God; the night also is Thine.

Thou makest the outgoings of the morning and evening to rejoice.

The eyes of all wait upon Thee, and Thou givest them their meat in due season.

Thou satisfiest the desire of every living thing.

Thou hast established the borders of the earth; Thou hast made winter and summer.

While the earth remaineth, seed-time and harvest, and cold and heat, and summer and winter, and day and night, shall not cease.

Thou crownest the year with Thy goodness, and Thy paths drop fatness.

They drop upon the pastures of the wilderness, and the little hills rejoice on every side.

The pastures are clothed with flocks: the valleys also are covered over with corn;

They shout for joy; they also sing.

Thou visitest the earth and waterest it;

Thou makest it soft with showers; Thou blessest the springing thereof.

Behold, the sons of men go forth to their labor, and the field yieldeth food for them and their children.

They reap every one his corn from the field; they gather every one his vintage from the vineyard.

Behold the fowls of the air: for they sow not, neither do they reap; yet your Heavenly Father feedeth them.

He giveth to the beast his food, and to the young ravens which cry.

He causeth the grass to grow for the cattle, and herb for the service of man.
He sendeth the springs into the valleys, which run among the hills.
The mountains and the hills break forth into singing;
And all the trees of the field clap their hands.
O Lord, how manifold are Thy works! in wisdom hast Thou made them all.
Who coverest Thyself with light as with a garment; who stretchest out the heavens like a curtain.

Oh, that men would praise the Lord for His goodness and for His wonderful works to the children of men!
Oh, bless our God, ye people, and make the voice of His praise to be heard!
The earth is full of the goodness of the Lord;
And His tender mercies are over all His works.
Bless the Lord, O my soul! and all that is within me bless His holy name!
I will sing to the Lord, as long as I live; I will sing praise to my God while I have my being.

VII. GLORIA.

ALL SING.

Glory be to the Father, who is in heav'n, the High and Ho-ly One!
As it was in the beginning, is now, and ev-er shall be, world with-out end. A-MEN.

VIII. RESPONSIVE READING AND SINGING.

LORD of the Harvest! Thee we hail!
    Thine ancient promise doth not fail:
The varying seasons haste their round;
With goodness all our years are crowned.

ALL SING.

God be thank'd for Har-vest! Let all the peo-ple say:

        Now everywhere Thy liberal hand
        Bestows new plenty o'er the land;
        Now sounds of music fill the air,
        As homeward all their treasures bear.

ALL SING.   God be thanked, etc.   [Music as before.]

        Lord of the Harvest! all is Thine:
        The rains that fall; the suns that shine;
        The seed once hidden in the ground;
        The skill that makes our fruits abound.

ALL SING.   God be thanked, etc.   [Music as before.]

        New every year Thy gifts appear,
        New praises from our lips shall sound;
        Our thanks we pay this holy day;
        Oh, let our hearts in tune be found!

ALL SING.   God be thanked, etc.   [Music as before.]

      IX. A CAROL MAY HERE BE SUNG.

      X. ADDRESSES, RECITATIONS, OR OTHER EXERCISES.

      XI. ANOTHER CAROL OR APPROPRIATE HYMN MAY BE SUNG.

      XII. DOXOLOGY, OR CLOSING HYMN OF PRAISE.

XIII. The Dismission.

We praise Thee, O God; we acknowledge Thee to be the Lord.

ALL SING.

All the earth doth worship Thee, the Father everlasting.

ALL SING. [Music as before.]

XIV. Benediction.

The Lord bless us and keep us. The Lord make His face to shine upon us, and be gracious to us. The Lord lift up His countenance upon us and give us peace.

ALL SING.

Fifth Special Service.

CHRISTMAS.

I. Organ Voluntary.

II Responsive Reading.

BEHOLD, I send my messenger before thy face, who shall prepare thy way before thee; the voice of one crying in the wilderness: Prepare ye the way of the Lord; make His paths straight.

Thou, child, shalt be called the Prophet of the Highest.

And he shall go before him in the spirit and power of Elias, to turn the hearts of the fathers to the children, and the disobedient to the wisdom of the just; to make ready a people prepared for the Lord.

Thou shalt go before the face of the Lord, to prepare His ways.

But the Lord shall arise; the glory of the Lord shall be revealed; all flesh shall see it together.

For the mouth of the Lord hath spoken it.

Behold, the days come, saith the Lord, that I will make a new covenant with you. I will put my law within you, and write it in your hearts.

And ye shall all know me, from the least even unto the greatest.

III. Anthem.—"Comfort ye my People."

IV. READING AND RESPONSES.

HOW beautiful upon the mountains are the feet of him that bringeth good tidings, that publisheth peace, that bringeth good tidings of good, that publisheth salvation, that saith unto Zion, Thy God reigneth!

ALL SING.

Arise, shine! for thy light is come, and the glory of the Lord is risen upon thee; and the Gentiles shall come to thy light, and kings to the brightness of thy rising.

ALL SING. Hallelujah, etc. [Music as before.]

Break forth into joy, sing together, ye waste places of Jerusalem! for the Lord hath comforted His people, and all the ends of the earth shall see the salvation of our God.

ALL SING. Hallelujah, etc. [Music as before.]

Rejoice greatly, O daughter of Zion! Behold, thy King cometh unto thee! He is the righteous Saviour; he shall speak peace unto the heathen; and his dominion shall be from sea to sea.

ALL SING. Hallelujah, etc. [Music as before.]

The spirit of the Lord God is upon him. The Lord anointed him to preach good tidings unto the meek. He sent him to bind up the broken-hearted; to proclaim liberty to the captives; to proclaim the acceptable year of the Lord; to comfort all who mourn; to give unto them beauty for ashes, the oil of joy for mourning, the garment of praise for the spirit of heaviness.

ALL SING. Hallelujah, etc. [Music as before.]

So prophets, moved by the Holy Spirit, spoke of the coming of the Messiah; looking toward the dawning of the Sun of Righteousness, who should arise with healing in his wings.

ALL SING. Hallelujah, etc. [Music as before.]

V. A CHRISTMAS ANTHEM OR CAROL.

VI. RESPONSIVE CANTICLE.

LO! at length the true Light, —
 Light for every man born into the world!
  Kindling the face of them that receive it,
  Till they become the sons of God.
Cease, blinding glories of the heavens,
Which none could see and live!
  Cease, gross darkness of the earth,
  Where the righteous put forth their hands and fear!
The veil between is taken away,
  And the mingling dayspring comes.
No longer is the dwelling of Eternal Life too bright above,
And the perishable world too dark below.
  The Son of God hath dwelt among us,
  Full of grace and truth.
The Son of man hath gone up on high,
Made perfect, through suffering, for the Holy of Holies.
  In him we have access by one spirit to the Father.
O Lord Almighty, Thy thoughts are not as our thoughts;
  But Thou hast looked on us with the pity of a man,
  And raised us to think the thoughts of God.
We had said, Our righteousness reacheth not unto Thee,
Or to the holy ones of Thy presence;
  But Thou hast made one family there and here,
  One living communion of seen and unseen.
We had said, Thou layest men fast in everlasting sleep;
  But, lo! they sleep unto everlasting waking.
Blessed be the Lord God, that giveth beauty for ashes,
  And the garment of praise for the spirit of heaviness.

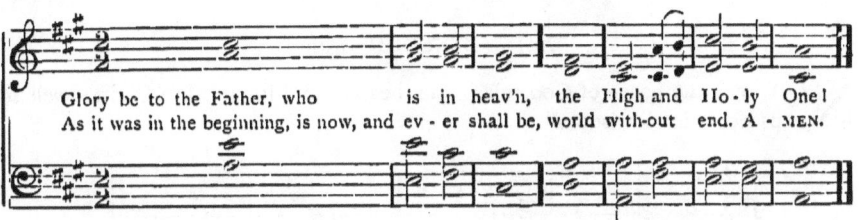

Glory be to the Father, who is in heav'n, the High and Ho-ly One!
As it was in the beginning, is now, and ev-er shall be, world with-out end. A-MEN.

VII. HYMN OR CAROL.

VIII. PRAYER.

FATHER of all, Thou hast never left the world without witness of Thyself. Thou hast always given men rain from heaven and fruitful seasons, filling their hearts with joy and gladness. But Thou hast blessed Thy children with food for the soul as well as for the body. Thou hast spoken to them by the still small voice of conscience. Holy men of old, whom Thou didst inspire, proclaimed Thy truth. And in the fulness of time Thou didst send Thy Son Jesus Christ into the world, to bring to men glad tidings of great joy, and to show the way which leads to everlasting peace. We praise Thee for the heavenly light of his teachings, and for the spirit of goodness which was the glory of his life. The path of duty which he pointed out is bright with the shining of his own blessed feet. Oh, may we who are taught the truth as it is in Jesus follow in his steps, — in lowliness of mind, in devotion to Thy will and to the good of Thy children, in a readiness to sacrifice all things for the sake of truth and right! So may his spirit be our spirit, giving us strength to shun every form of evil, and amidst all temptations to cleave to Thy most holy law.

These things we ask as his disciples. AMEN.

IX. CAROL.

X. ADDRESS OR RECITATIONS.

XI. CLOSING HYMN OR CAROL.

XII. Benedictions.

Now may the peace of God rule in our hearts; and the word of Christ dwell in us richly in all wisdom.

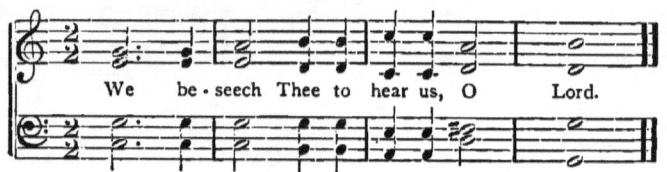

We beseech Thee to hear us, O Lord.

May our hearts repeat the song of the angels: "Glory to God in the highest; on earth peace, good-will to men!"

All sing. [Music as before.]

May the kingdom of God come in all the earth; and may His will be done here as it is in heaven.

Graciously hear us, O God. Amen.

Sixth Special Service.

EASTER.

I. Organ Voluntary.

II. Introductory Sentences.

AS the earth bringeth forth her bud, and the garden causeth the things sown in it to spring forth, so the Lord will cause righteousness and praise to spring forth among all nations.

Unto them who mourn He giveth beauty for ashes, the oil of joy for sorrowing, the garment of praise for the robes of heaviness.

Sing, O Heavens, and be joyful, O Earth, for the Lord hath comforted His people.

III. Hymn.

IV. Responsive Reading.

THE Lord shall comfort Zion.
   He will comfort all her waste places.
He will make her wilderness like Eden, and her desert like the garden of the Lord.
   Joy and gladness will be found therein, thanksgiving and the voice of melody.
The sun shall be no more thy light by day;
   Neither for brightness shall the moon give her light:
But the Lord shall be thine everlasting light, and thy God the glory.
   The Lord shall be thy strength and thy consolation.
The eternal God is thy refuge; and underneath are the everlasting arms.
   He will swallow up death in victory; and the Lord God will wipe off tears from all faces.

Whither shall I go from Thy spirit? or whither shall I flee from Thy presence?

If I ascend up into heaven, Thou art there; if I make my bed in the grave, behold Thou art there.

I am continually with thee; Thou hast holden me by my right hand.

Thou shalt guide me by Thy counsel, and afterward receive me to glory.

ALL SING.

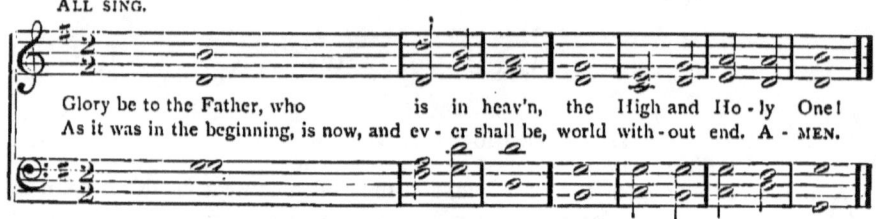

Glory be to the Father, who is in heav'n, the High and Ho-ly One!
As it was in the beginning, is now, and ev-er shall be, world with-out end. A-MEN.

V. CAROL.

VI. RESPONSIVE READING.

I AM the Resurrection and the Life, said Jesus: he that believeth on me, though he die, yet shall he live; and whosoever liveth and believeth on me shall never die.

I am the way, and the truth, and the life.

I am the living bread which came down out of heaven: if any man eat of this bread, he shall live forever.

Because I live, ye shall live also.

I am the vine; ye are the branches.

Abide in me, and I in you.

As touching the resurrection of the dead, have ye not read that which God spake unto you, saying, "I am the God of Abraham, and the God of Isaac, and the God of Jacob"?

God is not the God of the dead, but of the living; for all live unto Him.

If the dead rise not, then is not Christ raised.

ALL SING. *With spirit.*

But now is Christ ris-en from the dead.

For as in Adam all die, even so in Christ shall all be made alive.

ALL SING. *Softly.*

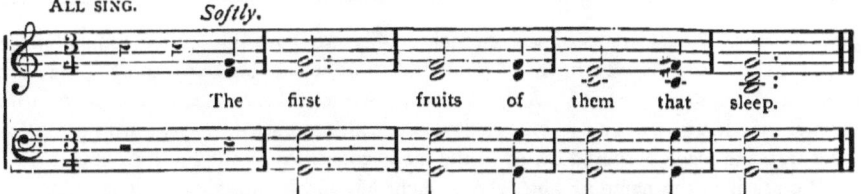

The first fruits of them that sleep.

For since by man came death, by man came also the resurrection of the dead.

ALL SING. *Joyful.*

For now is Christ ris-en, for now is Christ ris-en from the dead.

Every man in his own order; Christ the first fruits.

ALL SING. *Soft and slow.*

The first fruits of them that sleep, of them that sleep.

VII. PRAYER.

O THOU who always hearest when Thy children pray, we seek Thy guidance and implore Thy grace. Thou art the good Giver of every good gift; and we rejoice in giving Thee praise for all Thy benefits. We thank Thee for the coming of the Spring; for the fresh life which begins to glow in all things around us, and which will soon make itself known, — in the singing of the brooks and the birds, in the sweetness of flowers, in the garment of living green which the awakened earth puts on. But we thank Thee more that there is a fairer world than this, where everlasting Spring abides, — a land whose beauty never fades, a home that sorrows never dim.

And so with glad and grateful hearts we would keep this feast-day of the Prince of Life. We thank Thee that in him Thou givest us the victory over death and the grave, — the blessed hope of life eternal. May we have in tender remembrance to-day all the dear ones who have gone before us to the heavenly home. May our love for them never change. May we so live that our hearts shall be in union with their glorified spirits. And when our days on earth are ended, may we with great joy enter into the place prepared for us in the many mansions of our Father's house.

We ask it in the name of him who brought life and immortality to light. AMEN.

VIII. CAROL.

IX. ADDRESS OR RECITATIONS.

X. CLOSING HYMN OR CAROL.

XI. THE BLESSING.

THE Lord preserve our going out and our coming in, from this time forth and even for evermore.

[Or this:]

Blessing and honor, glory and power, be unto Him that sitteth upon the throne, and unto the Lamb.

Seventh Special Service.

FLORAL.

For "Children's Day," or any other Sunday in Summer. With or without Christening Service.

I. Responsive Reading.

Lo, the winter is past; the rain is over and gone;
The flowers appear on the earth; the time of the singing of birds is come.
The orchards put forth their green fruit.
The vines in blossom give forth fragrance.
Consider the lilies of the field, how they grow; they toil not, neither do they spin.
Yet Solomon in all his glory was not arrayed like one of these.

II. Hymn.

III. Prayer.

O LORD of heaven and earth, we bless Thee for Thy gracious bounty. In this summer season of fulness and plenty, Thou dost scatter Thy blessings with an open hand, making even the way-sides and lonely places rich with beauty. Thou art our Father; and, with the reverence and wonder of adoring children, we behold Thy works and seek to know Thy ways. Thy life gives to the flowers their grace and their beauty; and we hear Thy voice in the songs of the birds, in the gentle breezes, and the flowing waters. May we gain a double blessing from this Festival of Flowers, — the blessing of beauty, and the blessing of holy teaching. Gracious Father, there are flowers that may be opened within our hearts, — fair blossoms of fidelity, and charity, and peace. Shine upon us by Thy light, that these graces of character may give forth their fragrance. May the uprising of the fruits of the earth be a token of that uprising of the divine life which Thy Holy Spirit awakens. May no outward thing pass from our sight till it has filled our minds with some new lesson of wisdom and of goodness. So may the mind of Christ be formed within us, and Thy kingdom come in all our hearts. AMEN.

IV. CAROL OR SONG.

V. RESPONSIVE READING.

BLESS the Lord, O my soul! O Lord my God, Thou art very great; Thou art clothed with glory and majesty.

He covereth Himself with light, as with a garment; He spreadeth out the heavens like a curtain.

He layeth the beams of His chambers in the waters; He maketh the clouds His chariot; He rideth upon the wings of the wind.

He maketh the winds His messengers; the flaming lightnings His ministers.

He sendeth forth the springs in brooks; they run among the mountains.

About them the birds of heaven have their habitation; they sing among the branches.

He causeth grass to spring up for cattle, and herbage for the service of man.

The trees of the Lord are full of sap, the cedars of Lebanon which He hath planted.

O Lord, how manifold are Thy works! In wisdom hast Thou made them all.

The glory of the Lord shall endure forever; the Lord shall rejoice in His works.

I will sing to the Lord as long as I live; I will sing praise to my God while I have my being.

May my meditation be acceptable to Him! I will rejoice in the Lord.

VI. SONG OR CAROL.

VII. ADDRESS OR RECITATIONS.

VIII. CLOSING HYMN.

IX. BENEDICTION.

THE Lord bless us and keep us; the Lord make His face to shine upon us, and be gracious unto us; the Lord lift up the light of His countenance upon us and give us peace.

SUNDAY SCHOOL SERVICES. 85

When the Christening of Children is combined with this Service, the following may be used before the Benediction: —

SONG. — "HEAVENLY SHEPHERD, WHO ART FEEDING."

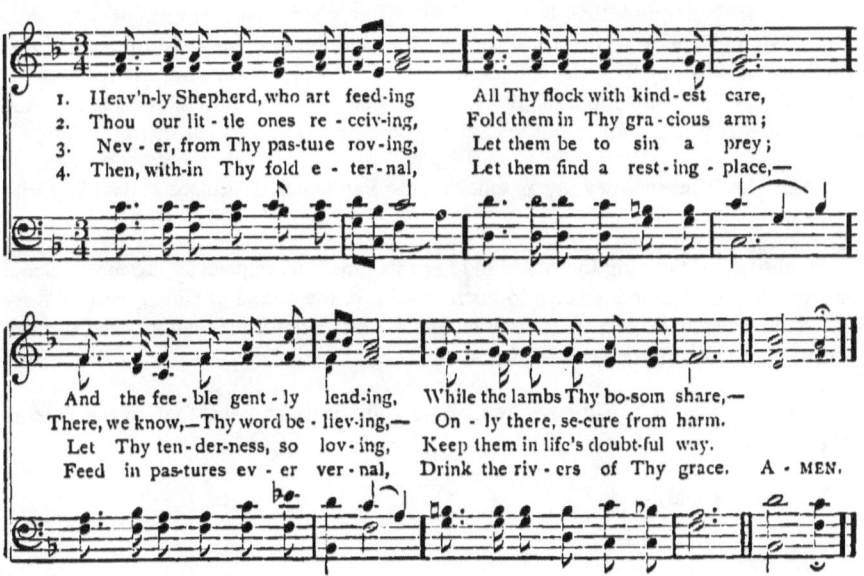

1. Heav'n-ly Shepherd, who art feeding   All Thy flock with kind-est care,
2. Thou our lit-tle ones re-ceiv-ing,   Fold them in Thy gra-cious arm;
3. Nev-er, from Thy pas-ture rov-ing,   Let them be to sin a prey;
4. Then, with-in Thy fold e-ter-nal,   Let them find a rest-ing-place,—

And the fee-ble gent-ly lead-ing,   While the lambs Thy bo-som share,—
There, we know,—Thy word be-liev-ing,—   On-ly there, se-cure from harm,
Let Thy ten-der-ness, so lov-ing,   Keep them in life's doubt-ful way.
Feed in pas-tures ev-er ver-nal,   Drink the riv-ers of Thy grace. A-MEN.

While the School is singing this song, the children may be brought forward for baptism. At the conclusion of the Christening ceremony, the School and Congregation may join in singing an appropriate

HYMN.

Then shall follow the

BENEDICTION.

For the convenience of those who use this book, the following brief form is given for the

CHRISTENING OF CHILDREN.

All those who are present standing up, the Minister shall say:

HEAR the words from the Gospel of Mark, in the tenth chapter, at the thirteenth verse:

They brought young children to Christ, that he should touch them; and his disciples rebuked those that brought them. But when Jesus saw it, he was much displeased, and said unto them, Suffer the little children to come unto me, and forbid them not; for of such is the kingdom of God. Verily I say unto you, whosoever shall not receive the kingdom of God as a little child, he shall not enter therein. And he took them up in his arms, put his hands upon them, and blessed them.

Then the Minister may say as follows; the Parents or Guardians responding with "AMEN."

By the act of bringing this Child here at this time, you express in the most solemn manner your desire and resolve to instruct *him* in the gospel of Christ, and in every way to do what lieth in you to enable *him* to resist sinful inclinations, and to keep God's holy will and commandments. AMEN.

Then the Minister shall take the Child into his arms, and shall say to the Parents or Guardians:

Name this Child.

Then shall he say:

This water is an emblem of the purity which Christ desires in the souls of all those who come to him.

And, naming the Child, he shall apply the water in the usual way, saying:

I baptize thee in the name of the Father, and of the Son, and of the Holy Spirit.

Or:

We dedicate thee to God; to the keeping of His love; to the service of His righteousness and truth.

Then shall follow the

Prayer.

HOLY Father, the heaven of Thy love lies about us in our infancy. Thy tender care watches over us in the days of our youth. Thy blessing always descends upon childlike hearts, for of such is Thy kingdom. In joyful confidence we bring our children unto Thee, giving what Thou hast given. May they grow up in the love of all that is worthy and good. May every thought and work and word be given to Thee; that life may be Thy service, and death the gate of heaven. AMEN.

Infant Class Services.

FIRST SERVICE.

ALL the Infant Classes being assembled, the Principal of the Primary Department shall conduct the Service. The Roll may be called. Then shall follow

THE GREETING.

The Teacher may recite the following, or any other selected verse; or the verse may be recited in concert:

KIND hearts are the gardens,
    Kind thoughts are the roots;
Kind words are the blossoms,
Kind deeds are the fruits.

Then may follow the

SONG.—"CAREFUL GARDENER."

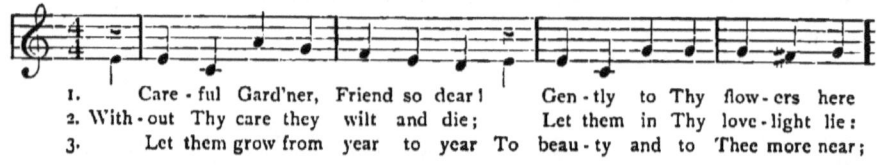

1. Care-ful Gard'ner, Friend so dear! Gen-tly to Thy flow-ers here
2. With-out Thy care they wilt and die; Let them in Thy love-light lie:
3. Let them grow from year to year To beau-ty and to Thee more near;

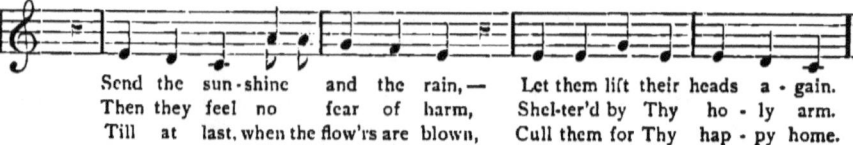

Send the sun-shine and the rain,— Let them lift their heads a-gain.
Then they feel no fear of harm, Shel-ter'd by Thy ho-ly arm.
Till at last, when the flow'rs are blown, Cull them for Thy hap-py home.

Here let all join in

THE PRAYER.

DEAR Father in heaven! we, a little band of children, have come to this Sunday School to learn what Thy will is, and how to do it. We have come from week-day lessons and play-hours, to pray and sing together, to study the Bible, and to learn how Thy dear Son Jesus grew in favor with God and man. Help us to make a good use of this quiet hour. May we not let our thoughts wander. May we attend to what our teachers say, and so do our part to make this a happy school. Bless our parents, our brothers and sisters, and all the rest, we pray Thee. AMEN.

Then shall be sung

THE HYMN. — GOD'S LOVE FOR LITTLE CHILDREN.

Music composed for this book by R. H. CLOUSTON, JR.

1. God the Father loves the children; Knows about their work and play;
2. God takes care of all the children, All the nights and all the days;
3. He will keep them, when they ask Him, Always patient, true, and mild;
4. By and by, for those who love Him, He will come some happy day,—

Helps them when they try to please Him; Hears them always when they pray.
Leads the little feet that follow In to Wisdom's pleasant ways.
Always pure and good and loving,— Each a happy little child.
Lead them to the pleasant pastures Of the land not far away.

Happy, happy little children! God the Father hears them pray!
Happy, happy little children! Led in Wisdom's pleasant ways!
Happy, happy little children! Always patient, true, and mild!
Oh, the happy little children, In the land not far away!

THE COLLECTION

May then be taken; and while one child is collecting the money, the following Questions and Answers may be said:

TEACHER. What did Jesus say about giving?
BOYS. "It is more blessed to give than to receive." Acts xx. 35.
TEACHER. What kind of a giver does God love?
GIRLS. "God loveth a cheerful giver." 2 Cor. ix. 7.
TEACHER. How have we received from God? and how should we give?
ALL. "Freely ye have received; freely give." Matt. x. 8.

Then may follow any

GENERAL LESSON.

After which the Classes may separate, and attend to the Class-Lessons.

CLOSE OF SCHOOL.

When the Classes come together again, they may first sing this

PRAYER – HYMN. — "FATHER, WE THANK THEE."

1. Can a lit-tle child like me Thank the Fa-ther fit-ting-ly?
2. For the fruit up-on the tree; For the birds that sing of Thee;

Yes, oh yes! be good and true, Pa-tient, kind in all you do;
For the earth in beau-ty dress'd; Fa-ther, moth-er, and the rest;

Love the Lord, and do your part; Learn to say, with all your heart:
For Thy ten-der, lov-ing care; For Thy boun-ty ev-'ry-where; —

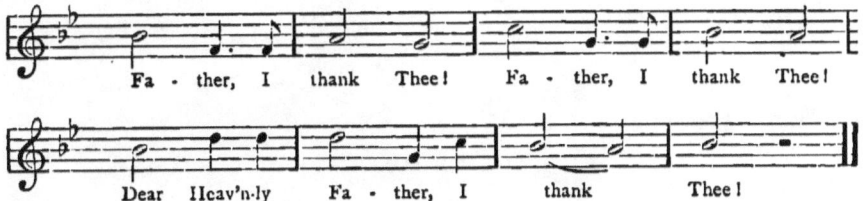

Then shall be said in concert

THE LORD'S PRAYER.

OUR Father, who art in heaven: Hallowed be Thy name. Thy kingdom come. Thy will be done on earth as it is in heaven. Give us this day our daily bread. And forgive us our trespasses, as we forgive those who trespass against us. And lead us not into temptation; but deliver us from evil. For Thine is the kingdom, and the power, and the glory, for ever and ever. AMEN.

Then may be added

THE BENEDICTION.

TEACHER. The Lord bless us and keep us.
ALL. The Lord make His face to shine upon us.
TEACHER. The Lord be gracious unto us, now and forevermore.
ALL. AMEN.

SECOND SERVICE.

The service may begin with

THE GREETING.

NOW to our loving Father, God,
    A gladsome song begin;
His light is on the world abroad,
    His joy our hearts within.
We turn to Him a smiling face,
    He smiles on us again;
He loves to see our cheerfulness
    And hear our thankful strain.

Then may be sung

A Hymn.

Then may be read

The Responses.

AND the child Samuel ministered unto the Lord before Eli. And it came to pass at that time that ere the lamp of God went out in the temple of the Lord, where the ark of God was, and Samuel was laid down to sleep, that the Lord called Samuel.

And he answered, Here am I! And he ran unto Eli, and said, Here am I; for thou calledst me.

And he said, I called not; lie down again. And he went and lay down. And the Lord called yet again, Samuel!

And Samuel arose and went to Eli, and said, Here am I; for thou didst call me.

And Eli perceived that the Lord had called the child. And he said, If He call thee, thou shalt say, Speak, Lord, for Thy servant heareth. And the Lord came, and stood, and called as at other times, Samuel! Samuel!

Then Samuel answered, Speak, for Thy servant heareth.

The Collection

May then be taken; and while one child is collecting the money, the following Questions and Answers may be said:

Teacher. What did Jesus say about giving?
Boys. "It is more blessed to give than to receive." Acts xx. 35.
Teacher. What kind of a giver does God love?
Girls. "God loveth a cheerful giver." 2 Cor. ix. 7.
Teacher. How have we received from God? and how should we give?
All. "Freely ye have received; freely give." Matt. x. 8.

When quiet is restored, then shall be said by all

The Prayer.

OUR Father, who art in heaven, and on the earth, Thou art the source of life; Thou art the giver of every good. Thou hast taught us to look to Thee in prayer, and to worship Thee in spirit and in truth. We are the children of Thy love. As we grow in years, may we grow in grace and in all wisdom. Thou speakest to our hearts; and often do we hear the voice within, which tells us to do the right and shun the wrong. May we always be awake to hear Thy call and to do Thy will. May the lessons of virtue which are taught us here sink into our souls, and bear much fruit in our lives. Be Thou so near us that evil may be far off; so dear to us that we may ever love Thee, with mind and heart and soul and strength. AMEN.

Then may be sung

A HYMN.

Then may follow any

GENERAL LESSON.

After which the Classes may separate, and attend to the Class-Lessons.

For the Closing Exercises, see First Service.

THIRD SERVICE.

The Service may begin with

THE GREETING.

A GLADSOME hymn of praise we sing;
    And thankfully we gather,
To bless the love of God above,
    Our Everlasting Father.
In Him rejoice, with heart and voice,
    Whose glory fadeth never;
Whose providence is our defence;
    Who lives and loves forever.

Then may be sung

A HYMN.

Then may be read

THE RESPONSES.

HEARKEN unto the voice of my cry, my King, and my God;
    For unto Thee will I pray.
My voice shalt Thou hear in the morning, O Lord:
    In the morning will I direct my prayer unto Thee, and will look up.
The Lord hath heard my supplication;
    The Lord will receive my prayer.

The Collection

May then be taken; and while one child is collecting the money, the following Questions and Answers may be said:

TEACHER. What did Jesus say about giving?
BOYS. "It is more blessed to give than to receive." Acts xx. 35.
TEACHER. What kind of a giver does God love?
GIRLS. "God loveth a cheerful giver." 2 Cor. ix. 7.
TEACHER. How have we received from God? and how should we give?
ALL. "Freely ye have received; freely give." Matt. x. 8.

When quiet is restored, there shall be said by all

The Prayer.

OUR Father, who art in heaven! we are so young we cannot do much; but we want to do all we can. The birds build nests, the ants hills, the bees cells. We wish to be busy, too, and to be kind in all our work. Help us to earn something to give to children who are poorer than we are. Help us to be willing to share our books and toys with those who have few. May we not be selfish. May we be kind to all animals. May we be obedient to our parents and teachers. May we have smiles, kind words, kind thoughts, for all. Dear Father, help us to remember that what we have is given us to share. May we follow Jesus, and be Thy true and loving children. AMEN.

Then may be sung

A Hymn.

Then may follow any

General Lesson.

After which the Classes may separate, and attend to the Class-Lessons.

For the Closing Exercises, see First Service.

HYMNAL

FOR

THE SUNDAY SCHOOL.

PREFACE.

THIS HYMNAL, which has been prepared to supply a long-felt need, contains gleanings from many scattered fields of poetry and music. The aim has been to select only such hymns as are characterized by simplicity and purity of language. If any of the selections fall below this standard, it is because the sentiment of the hymns, or their union with good tunes, has been deemed a sufficient reason for retaining them; but the Editor has kept in mind the importance of making children familiar with such hymns as they can love and value all their lives. Many noble poems of a lyrical character are here for the first time set to equally noble tunes, and thus added to the available Hymnology of the Sunday School. In adapting hymns to music, the Editor has not hesitated to alter phraseology whenever by so doing he could present a hymn in a form better fitted to the uses of those schools for which this book has been specially compiled.

Of the tunes it may be said that the plan has been to provide pleasing melodies, such as children like to sing, and at the same time "to secure the sound harmonies which shall accustom their ears to what is good." Some pieces of less musical merit have been admitted, which may serve as stepping-stones to the better tunes. With a proper amount of practice under an inspiring leader, children of average musical training can be taught to sing the best tunes; and their enjoyment of such compositions — provided the melody is clearly and fully defined — is as keen and as lasting as the pleasure which they take in learning and reciting the best poetry.

The tunes here presented include selections from the works of several of the best modern composers of the English school, arrangements and adaptations from German music of acknowledged excellence, and some original pieces contributed by American composers. A number of old chorals and standard hymn-tunes used by the churches are given because of their intrinsic value, and also to prepare the children to take part in congregational singing. A special feature of the book is the limitation of each tune to a single hymn. The effect of such association, where words and music are well matched, is to fix both the hymn and the tune in the memory, and to make of them the strong wings on which aspiration may soar heavenward.

Acknowledgment is made to Messrs. Houghton, Mifflin, & Co. for permission to use four of Whittier's hymns; to Messrs. O. Ditson & Co. for use of the Carol, No. 185; to W. W. Huntington for permission to copy from the "Children's Hymnal" tune No. 15; to Professor F. L. Ritter for his song, "Evening Prayer" (No. 41); and to Rev. Phillips Brooks and Mr. L. P. Redner for the words and music of the Christmas Carol, No. 198. Cordial thanks are due to the many friends who have sent or suggested hymns and tunes, and also to others who have written tunes expressly for this Hymnal. The Editor is under special obligations to Mr. R. H. Clouston, Jr., and Mr. E. H. Bailey for their original compositions, and to Mr. Bailey for constant assistance and advice in the arrangement of harmonies and correction of proofs.

TABLE OF CONTENTS.

	HYMN
PRAISE	1–24
SUNDAY	25–32
CLOSE OF SERVICE	33–39
EVENING	40–41
GOD IN NATURE	42–59
RELIGION OF CHILDHOOD	60–78
PROCESSIONAL	79–85
MINISTRY OF JESUS	86–106
GOD'S CARE AND LOVE	107–118
PRAYER AND TRUST	119–135
WARFARE OF LIFE	136–149
GOOD WORKS	150–160
HEAVEN AND HEAVENLY COMFORT	161–171
INFANT CLASS SONGS	172–177
FESTIVAL SONGS:	
ANNIVERSARY	178–179
EASTER	180–183
FLORAL	184–186
NATIONAL	187–188
HARVEST	189–193
CHRISTMAS	194–198

SUNDAY SCHOOL HYMNAL.

PRAISE.

2. DYKES. 8s & 7s.
Bp. Richard Mant.   *Rev. J. B. Dykes.*

1. "Lord, Thy glo-ry fills the heav-en; Earth is with its ful-ness stored;
   Un-to Thee be glo-ry giv-en, Ho-ly, ho-ly, ho-ly Lord!"
2. Heav'n is still with an-thems ring-ing; Earth takes up the an-gels' cry:
   "Ho-ly, ho-ly, ho-ly," singing, "Lord of Hosts, the Lord Most High!" A-MEN.

After last verse.

3 With His seraph train before Him,
   With His holy Church below,
   Thus unite we to adore Him,
   Did we thus our anthem flow:

4 "Lord, Thy glory fills the heaven;
   Earth is with its fulness stored;
   Unto Thee be glory given,
   Holy, holy, holy Lord!" AMEN.

3. LOWESTOFT. 7s.
Rev. C. B. Taylor.   *F. A. Mann.*

1. Let us sing!—the an-gels sing, High a-bove the cloud-less sky,
   Where they see their heav'n-ly King In his ho-ly maj-es-ty.
2. Let us sing!—the chil-dren sang, When to Si-on Je-sus came;
   And the state-ly tem-ple rang With ho-san-nas to his name. A-MEN.

After last verse.

3 Let us sing! rejoice, rejoice!
   God will listen while we sing;
   Praise Him with the heart and voice,
   And to Him our tribute bring.

4 Let us sing our hymns below,—
   Sing at morn, at noon, at ev'n;
   Till at last in peace we go,
   Sweeter songs to sing in heav'n. AMEN.

PRAISE.

4. J. MONTGOMERY.   INNOCENTS. 7s.   W. H. MONK.

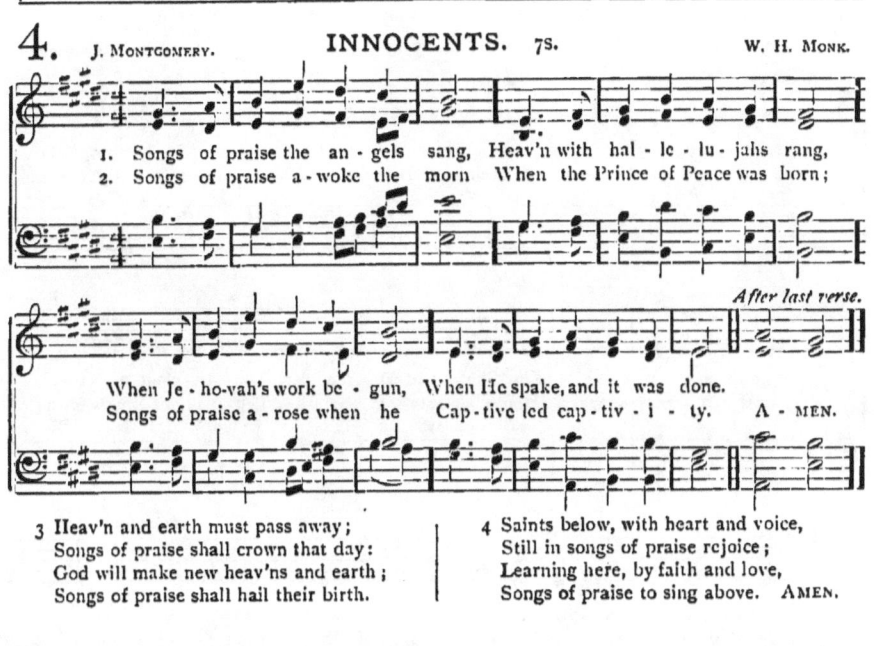

1. Songs of praise the an-gels sang, Heav'n with hal-le-lu-jahs rang,
When Je-ho-vah's work be-gun, When He spake, and it was done.

2. Songs of praise a-woke the morn When the Prince of Peace was born;
Songs of praise a-rose when he Cap-tive led cap-tiv-i-ty. A-MEN.

After last verse.

3 Heav'n and earth must pass away;
  Songs of praise shall crown that day:
  God will make new heav'ns and earth;
  Songs of praise shall hail their birth.

4 Saints below, with heart and voice,
  Still in songs of praise rejoice;
  Learning here, by faith and love,
  Songs of praise to sing above. AMEN.

5.   CHILDREN'S PRAISE. 7s & 6s.   German.

1. O Lord, while an-gels praise Thee, And all cre-a-tion sings,
To Thee, al-might-y Spir-it, My soul its trib-ute brings.

2. The morn-ing stars all praise Thee, The heav'n-ly host on high,
The beams of ear-ly dawn-ing, And pur-ple ev'n-ing sky.

3 But Thou dost gladly listen
  To hear Thy children sing;
  Thou wilt accept the praises
  Which unto Thee they bring.

4 To Thee I give my being,
  I consecrate my days;
  And ev'ry day my duty
  Shall be to live Thy praise.

PRAISE.

6. Sir R. Grant.   HANOVER. 5 5. 5 5. 6 5. 6 5.   Dr. Croft

1. Oh, wor-ship the King All glo-rious a-bove! Oh, grate-ful-ly sing His pow'r and His love! Our Shield and De-fen-der, The An-cient of Days, Pa-vil-ion'd in splen-dor, And gird-ed with praise!

2. Oh, tell of His might! Oh, sing of His grace! Whose robe is the light, Whose can-o-py space; His char-iots of wrath The thun-der-clouds form; And dark is His path On the wings of the storm! A-MEN.

After last verse.

3 Thy bountiful care
  What tongue can recite?
It breathes in the air,
It shines in the light;
It streams from the hills,
It descends to the plain,
And sweetly distils
  In the dew and the rain.

4 Frail children of dust,
  And feeble as frail,
In Thee do we trust,
Nor find Thee to fail.
Thy mercies how tender!
How firm to the end!
Our Maker, Defender,
  Redeemer, and Friend! AMEN.

7. S. C. Clarke.   MORNING LIGHT. 5 5. 10. 5 5. 10.   Rev. J. B. Dykes.

1. Fram-er of the light, Who from out the night The dawn of

PRAISE.

2 By Thy mercy still
  Spared our place to fill,
O Father, be it ours Thy name to bless;
  Shelter'd by Thy pow'r,
  In each fleeting hour
Thy children guide to paths of holiness.

3 Onward to the goal
  Lead each striving soul,
Upheld by strength divine Thy grace supplies;
  While it still is day,
  May we win our way   [AMEN.
Towards the mark and our high calling's prize.

8.   "COME, HAPPY CHILDREN!" C.M.   HENRY LAHEE.

3 Sing of the wonders of His truth,
  And read in ev'ry page
The promise made to earliest youth
  Fulfill'd to latest age!

4 Sing of the wonders of His pow'r,
  Who with His own right arm
Upholds and keeps you hour by hour,
  And shields from ev'ry harm!

PRAISE.

9. Bp. Heber.   NICÆA. P.M.   Rev. J. B. Dykes.

1. Holy, holy, holy! Lord God Almighty! Early in the morning our song shall rise to Thee; Holy, holy, holy! merciful and mighty! All Thy works shall praise Thy name in earth, and sky, and sea!

    2 Holy, holy, holy! all the saints adore Thee,
      Casting down their golden crowns around the glassy sea;
      Cherubim and seraphim falling down before Thee,
      Thou who wast, and art, and evermore shalt be!

    3 Holy, holy, holy! though the darkness hide Thee,
      Though the eye of sinful man Thy glory may not see,
      Only Thou art holy, there is none beside Thee,
      Infinite in pow'r, in love, and purity!

10. Rev. E. Caswall.   NOMEN. 6s.   J. Barnby.

1. When morning gilds the skies, My heart awaking cries,
2. When-e'er the sweet church-bell Peals over hill and dell,

PRAISE.

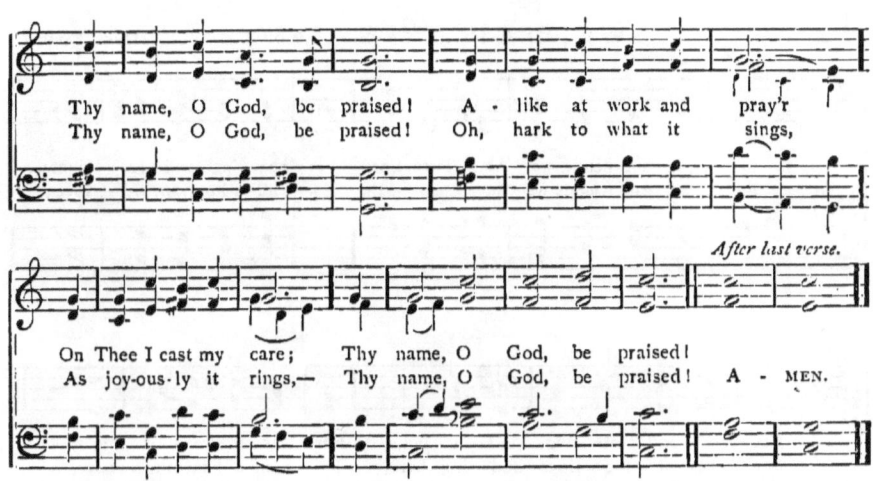

Thy name, O God, be praised! A-like at work and pray'r On Thee I cast my care; Thy name, O God, be praised!
Thy name, O God, be praised! Oh, hark to what it sings, As joy-ous-ly it rings,— Thy name, O God, be praised! A-MEN.

After last verse.

3 Does sadness fill my mind?
   A solace here I find,
      Thy name, O God, be praised!
   Or fades my earthly bliss?
   My comfort still is this,
      Thy name, O God, be praised!

4 In heav'n's eternal bliss
   The loveliest strain is this,
      Thy name, O God, be praised!
   Let earth, and sea, and sky,
   From depth to height reply,
      Thy name, O God, be praised! AMEN.

11. DOUGLAS WALMSLEY. INTEGER VITÆ. P.M. FLEMMING.

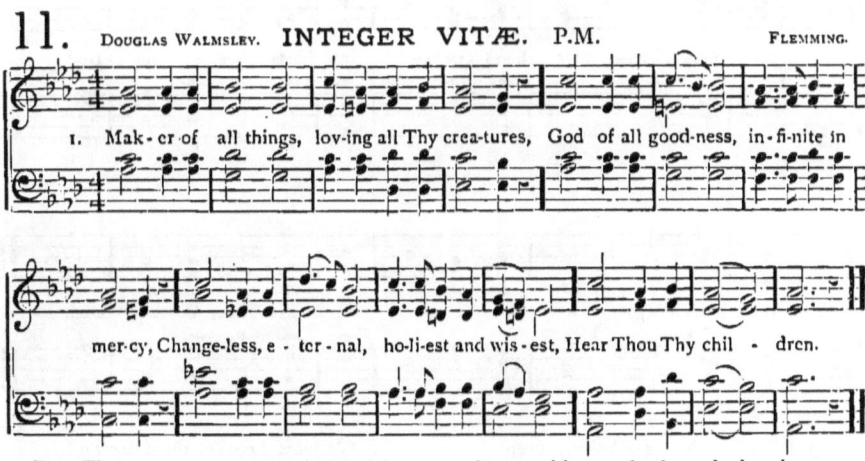

1. Mak-er of all things, lov-ing all Thy crea-tures, God of all good-ness, in-fi-nite in mer-cy, Change-less, e-ter-nal, ho-li-est and wis-est, Hear Thou Thy chil-dren.

2 Bless Thou our purpose, consecrate our labors;
   Keep us still faithful to the best and truest;
   Guide us, protect us, make us not unworthy
      Learners of Jesus.

3 Glory and honor, thanks and adoration,
   Still will we bring, O God of men and angels,
   To Thee, the holy, merciful, and mighty
      Father, our Father!

3 For all the founts of wisdom deep;
  That wisdom from above
  Thy Spirit gives each pray'rful soul
  To teach all truth and love, —
      We bless Thee, O our God.

4 We bless Thee for the dearest gift,
  Enjoyed or understood,
  The priceless gift to know and feel
  That Thou Thyself art good, —
      We bless Thee, O our God.

PRAISE.

13. Rev. S. C. Beach. SCHUMANN. L.M. Schumann.

1. Thou One in all, Thou All in one! Source of the grace that crowns our days!
For all Thy gifts 'neath cloud or sun, We lift to Thee our grate-ful praise.

2. We bless Thee for the life that flows A pulse in ev-'ry grain of sand,
A beau-ty in the blush-ing rose, A thought and deed in brain and hand.

3 For life that Thou hast made a joy,
   For strength to make our lives like Thine,
   For duties that our hands employ,—
    We bring our offerings to Thy shrine.

4 Be Thine to give and ours to own
   The truth that sets Thy children free,
   The law that binds us to Thy throne,
   The love that makes us one with Thee.

14. WHO GIVEST ALL. 8.8.8.4. Rev. J. B. Dykes.

1. O Lord of heav'n, and earth, and sea, To Thee all praise and glo-ry be;
2. The gold-en sun-shine, ver-nal air, Sweet flow'rs and fruit, Thy love de-clare;
3. For peace-ful homes and health-ful days, For all the bless-ings earth dis-plays,

After last verse.

How shall we show our love to Thee, Who giv-est all?
When har-vests rip-en, Thou art there, Who giv-est all.
We owe Thee thank-ful-ness and praise, Who giv-est all. A-MEN.

4 Whatever, Lord, we give to Thee,
   Repaid a thousandfold will be;
   Then gladly will we lend to Thee,
    Who givest all.

5 To Thee, from whom we all derive
   Our life, our gifts, our power to give!
   Oh, may we ever with Thee live.
    Who givest all! AMEN.

PRAISE.

15. HEAVENLY SHEPHERD. 8s, 7s, & 4s. E. J. Hopkins.

1. Heav'n-ly Shepherd, true and holy, Hear, O hear us, while we pray! Let thy children, weak and lowly, Be thy care in life's young day. Heav'n-ly Shepherd! Hear thy children as they pray. A-MEN.

2 We are Thine; do Thou befriend us,
   Be the guardian of our way;
   Keep Thy flock, from sin defend us;
   Seek us when we go astray.
       Heavenly Shepherd!
   Hear us when we praise and pray!

3 Early let us seek Thy favor,
   Early let us do Thy will;
   Early follow Christ our Saviour,
   And his precepts e'er fulfil:
       Heavenly Shepherd!
   Thou hast blessed us — bless us still. AMEN.

PRAISE.

16. NEWPORT. 7s & 6s. D. A. R. Watson.

1. Once more to Thee, O Father, With thankful hearts we come;
From days of toil and pleasure, From many a happy home.
For all Thy countless blessings We praise Thy holy Name,
And own Thy love unchanging, Through days and years the same.

2 For all the dear affection
   Of parents, brothers, friends,
To Him our thanks we render
   Who these and all things sends.
But these, O Lord, can show us
   Thy goodness but in part;
Thy love would lead us onward
   To know Thee as Thou art.

3 Lord, gather all thy children
   To meet Thee at the last,
When earthly tasks are ended,
   And earthly days are past;
With all our dear ones round us
   In that eternal home,
Where death no more shall part us,
   And night shall never come!

3 O Lord, Thy heavenly truth
  Wilt Thou to us impart;
  And teach us in our youth
  To know Thee as Thou art.
    Alleluia!
  Then shall we sing
  To God our King:
    Alleluia!

4 Oh! may Thy holy word
  Spread all the world around;
  And all with one accord
  Uplift the joyful sound:
    Alleluia!
  All then shall sing
  To God their King:
    Alleluia!

PRAISE.

18. N. L. FROTHINGHAM.   ST. CRISPIN. L.M.   Sir G. J. ELVEY.

1. O God, whose presence glows in all Within, around us, and above!
Thy word we bless, Thy name we call, Whose word is Truth, whose name is Love.

2 That love its holy influence pour,
To keep us meek and make us free,
And throw its binding blessing more
Round each with all, and all with Thee.

3 Send down its angel to our side;
Send in its calm upon the breast:
For we would know no other guide,
And we can need no other rest.

19.   ST. PETER. C.M.   ALEXANDER ROBERT REINAGLE.

1. Now to our loving Father, God, A gladsome song begin;
His smile is on the world abroad, His joy our hearts within.
2. We need not, Lord, our gladness leave To worship Thee aright;
Our joyfulness for praise receive! Thou mak'st our lives so bright.

3 We turn to God a smiling face,
He smiles on us again;
He loves to see our cheerfulness,
And hear our gladsome strain.

4 The pure in heart are always glad,
The smile of God they feel:
He doth the secret of His joy
To blameless hearts reveal.

PRAISE.

20. MORNING. P. M. — Bullinger.

1. The morn-ing, the bright and the beau-ti-ful morn-ing Is up, and the sun-shine is all on the wing, With its fresh flush of glad-ness the land-scape a-dorn-ing, A glad-ness which noth-ing but morn-ing can bring.

2. And we too a-wake; for our kind, lov-ing Fa-ther, Who sooth'd us so gen-tly to sleep on His breast, And made the soft still-ness of ev'n-ing to gath-er A-round us, now calls us a-gain from our rest.

3 But, ere to our labors and duties returning,
We hasten to give Him the praise that is meet;
In solemn devotion, the hours of this morning,
Our freest and freshest, we lay at His feet.

4 Oh, then let us haste to our kind, loving Father,
And ere the fair skies of life's dawning be dim,
Let us come with glad hearts, let us come all together,—
The morn of our youth let us hallow to Him!

21. Lucy Larcom. FATHERHOOD. 8s, 7s, & 4s. — Henry Farmer.

1. We are chil-dren of one Fa-ther, All a-like His chil-dren dear;

PRAISE.

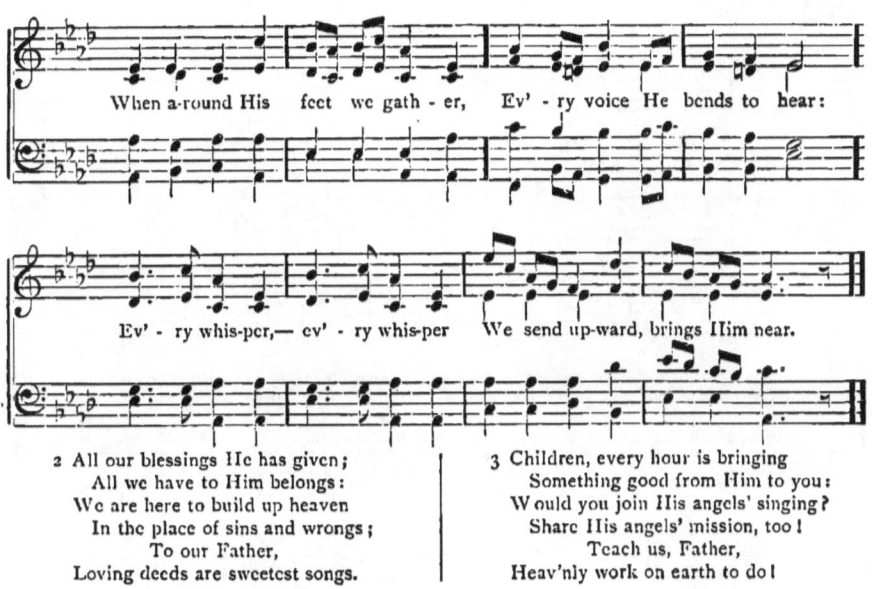

When a-round His feet we gath-er, Ev'-ry voice He bends to hear:
Ev'-ry whis-per,— ev'-ry whis-per We send up-ward, brings Him near.

2 All our blessings He has given;
All we have to Him belongs:
We are here to build up heaven
In the place of sins and wrongs;
To our Father,
Loving deeds are sweetest songs.

3 Children, every hour is bringing
Something good from Him to you:
Would you join His angels' singing?
Share His angels' mission, too !
Teach us, Father,
Heav'nly work on earth to do !

22. Spirit of the Psalms.   ANTIOCHIA. S. M.   PHILIP ARMES.

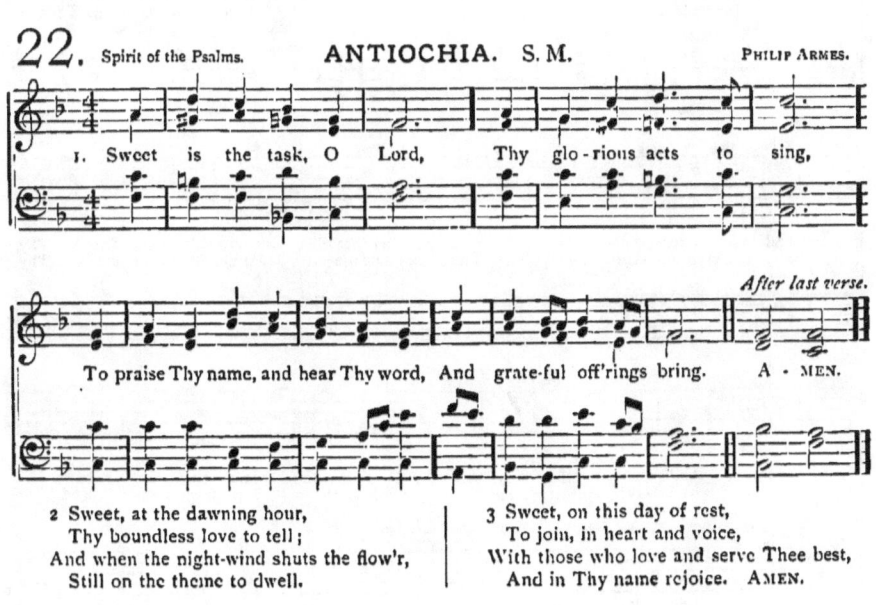

1. Sweet is the task, O Lord, Thy glo-rious acts to sing,
To praise Thy name, and hear Thy word, And grate-ful off'rings bring.   A - MEN.

After last verse.

2 Sweet, at the dawning hour,
Thy boundless love to tell;
And when the night-wind shuts the flow'r,
Still on the theme to dwell.

3 Sweet, on this day of rest,
To join, in heart and voice,
With those who love and serve Thee best,
And in Thy name rejoice.   AMEN.

2 Celebrate the eternal God
 With harp and psaltery,
 Timbrels soft and cymbals loud
 In His high praise agree:
 Praise Him every tuneful string;
 All the reach of heavenly art,
 All the powers of music bring,
 The music of the heart.

3 Him in whom they move and live
 Let every creature sing,
 Glory to their Maker give,
 And homage to their King:
 Hallowed be His name beneath,
 As in heaven on earth adored;
 Praise the Lord in every breath!
 Let all things praise the Lord!

SUNDAY.

25. Bp. Wordsworth. **DAY OF REST.** 7s & 6s. D. Dr. John Stainer.

1. Oh, day of rest and gladness! Oh, day of joy and light! Oh, balm of care and sadness! Most beautiful, most bright! On thee let mortals lowly Take up the angels' cry,— Sing Holy, holy, holy, To God the Lord Most High!

2 Oh, day of sweet refection,
Thou art a day of love!
Oh, day of resurrection
From earth to things above!
On thee, etc.

3 New graces ever gaining
From this our day of rest,
We reach the rest remaining
To spirits of the blest.
On thee, etc.

26. J. Ellerton. **SWABIA.** S. M. German.

Joyful.

1. This is the day of light,— Let there be light to-day!
2. This is the day of rest,— Our failing strength renew!

SUNDAY.

After last verse.

O Dayspring, rise up-on our night, And chase its gloom a-way!
On wear-y brain and troubled breast Shed Thou Thy fresh'ning dew!   A-MEN.

3 This is the day of peace, —
　Thy peace our spirits fill!
　Bid Thou the blasts of discord cease,
　The waves of strife be still!

4 This is the day of pray'r, —
　Let earth to heav'n draw near!
　Lift up our hearts to seek Thee there;
　Come down to meet us here!   AMEN.

27.   ANNA L. BARBAULD.   **LORD OF LIGHT.**   C. M.   MARSCHNER.

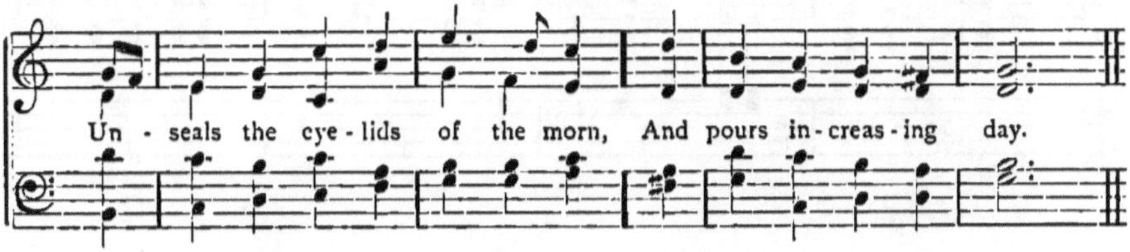

1. A-gain the Lord of life and light A-wakes the kind-ling ray;
Un-seals the eye-lids of the morn, And pours in-creas-ing day.
We praise Thee, we bless Thee, Thou Lord of life and light.

2 This day be grateful homage paid,
　And loud hosannas sung;
　Let gladness dwell in ev'ry heart,
　And praise on ev'ry tongue.
　We praise Thee, etc.

3 Ten thousand diff'ring lips shall join
　To hail this welcome morn,
　Which scatters blessings from its wings
　To nations yet unborn.
　We praise Thee, etc.

SUNDAY.

SUNDAY.

29. HERFORD. 8.6.8.4. E. S. Carter.

1. Hail, sa-cred day of earth-ly rest, From toil and trou-ble free!
2. A ho-ly still-ness, breath-ing calm On all the world a-round,

Hail, day of light, that bring-est light And joy to me!
Up-lifts my soul, O God, to Thee, Where rest is found. A-MEN.

After last verse.

3 No sound of jarring strife is heard,
As weekly labors cease;
No voice, but those that sweetly sing
Sweet songs of peace.

4 Accept, O God, my hymn of praise,
That Thou this day hast given:
Sweet foretaste of that endless day
Of rest in heaven. AMEN.

30. BEETHOVEN. 7s. BEETHOVEN.

1. In this peace-ful hour of pray'r, Strong-er faith, O God, we seek;
2. In our great-est tri-als we Calm thro' Thee the way have trod;

Here we bring each earth-ly care: Thou the strength'ning mes-sage speak!
In the small-est may we feel Thou art still our Help-er-God.

3 Of Thy presence and Thy love
We more constant feeling need,
Till the high and holy thought
Hallow ev'ry simplest deed.

4 In our work and in our homes
True and loving we would be;
Learn how daily life affords
Noblest opportunity.

SUNDAY.

31. ST. BEES. 7s.
Rev. J. B. Dykes.

1. Lord, this day Thy children meet
In Thy courts with willing feet;
Unto Thee this day they raise
Grateful hearts in hymns of praise.

2. Not alone the day of rest
With Thy worship shall be blest;
In our pleasure and our glee,
Lord, we would remember Thee. A-MEN.

After last verse.

3 Help us unto Thee to pray,
And to hallow ev'ry day;
From Thy presence thus to win
Hearts all pure and free from sin.

4 All our blessings here below,
Father, from Thy mercy flow;
All Thy children Thou dost love,—
Draw our hearts to Thee above. AMEN.

32. SACRED MORN. 7s.
Julia A. Elliott. *German.*

1. Hail, thou bright and sacred morn,
Ris'n with gladness in thy beams!
Light, which not of earth is born,
From thy dawn in glory streams.

2. Sad and weary were our way,
Fainting oft beneath our load,
But for thee, thou blessèd day,
Resting place on life's rough road.

3 Soon, too soon, the sweet repose
Of this holy day will cease;
Soon this glimpse of heav'n will close,
Vanish soon these hours of peace.

4 But the rest which yet remains
For Thy people, Lord, above,
Knows nor change, nor fears, nor pains,—
Endless as our Father's love.

CLOSE OF SERVICE.

33. J. ELLERTON.   PARTING. 10s.   E. J. HOPKINS.

1. Father, again to Thy dear name we raise
With one accord our parting hymn of praise;
We stand to bless Thee ere our worship cease,
Then, lowly kneeling, wait Thy word of peace.

2 Grant us Thy peace upon our homeward way;
With Thee began, with Thee shall end, the day;
Guard Thou the lips from sin, the hearts from shame,
That in this house have called upon Thy name.

3 Grant us Thy peace throughout our earthly life,
Our balm in sorrow and our stay in strife;
Then, when Thy voice shall bid our conflict cease,
Call us, O Lord, to Thine eternal peace!

34. W. C. BRYANT.   BRYANT. 7s.   JOHN ADCOCK.

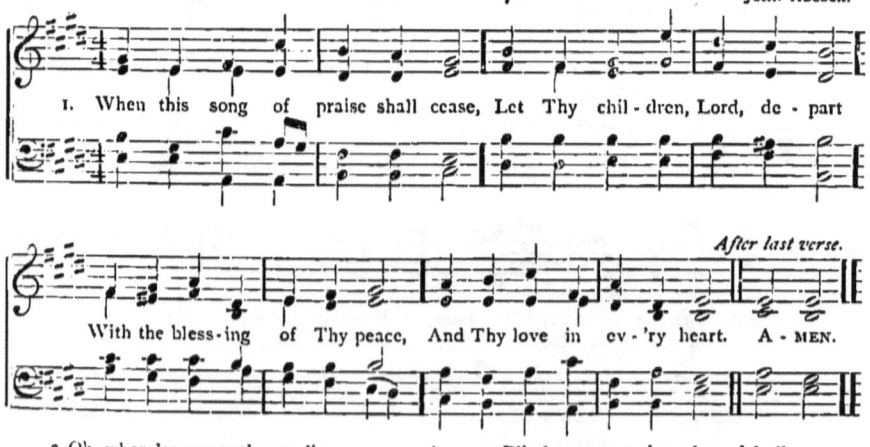

1. When this song of praise shall cease,
Let Thy children, Lord, depart
With the blessing of Thy peace,
And Thy love in ev'ry heart. A-MEN.

2 Oh, where'er our path may lie,
Father, let us not forget
That we walk beneath Thine eye,
That Thy care upholds us yet.

3 Blind are we, and weak, and frail;
Be Thine aid forever near;
May the fear to sin prevail
Over every other fear. AMEN.

CLOSE OF SERVICE.

37. F. W. FABER. ST. MATTHIAS. L. M. 6 lines. W. H. MONK.

1. Our Father, bless us ere we go; Thy word in-to our minds in-stil;
And make our lukewarm hearts to glow With low-ly love and fer-vent will.
Thro' life's long day and death's dark night, O lov-ing Fa-ther, be our Light! A-MEN.

After last verse.

2 Grant us, dear Lord, from evil ways
  Deliv'rance, pardon, and release;
And bless us, more than in past days,
  With purity and inward peace.
Thro' life's long day and death's dark night,
  O Loving Father, be our Light!

3 For all we love, — the poor, the sad,
  The sinful, — unto Thee we call;
Oh, let Thy mercy make us glad, —
  Thou art our Life, our Hope, our All.
Thro' life's long day and death's dark night,
  O loving Father, be our Light! AMEN.

38. ON OUR WAY REJOICING. 6s & 5s. D. F. R. HAVERGAL.

Joyous.

1. On our way re-joic-ing, As we home-ward move,

CLOSE OF SERVICE.

2 If with honest-hearted
   Love for God and man,
   Day by day Thou find us
   Doing what we can, —
   Thou who giv'st the seed-time
   Wilt give large increase,
   Crown the head with blessings,
   Fill the heart with peace.
      Chorus.

3 On our way rejoicing
   Gladly let us go;
   Conquer'd hath our leader,
   Vanquish'd is our foe!
   Loving cheer around us,
   Cheerful love within,
   Faith's good battle fighting,
   Vict'ry we shall win!
      Chorus.

CLOSE OF SERVICE.

39. Rev. S. J. Stone. **RENEWAL.** C. M. D. B. A. Weber.

1. An-oth-er week's cam-paign is o'er, Be-hold a new be-gun;
Not yet is closed the ho-ly war, Not yet the tri-umph won.
Not yet the end, not yet re-pose; We hear our Cap-tain say,
"Go forth a-gain to meet your foes, Ye chil-dren of the day!"

2 "Go forth, firm faith in every heart,
 Bright hope on every helm;
Through that shall pierce no fiery dart,
 And this no fear o'erwhelm.
Go in the spirit and the might
 Of him who led the way;
Close with the legions of the night,
 Ye children of the day!"

3 So forth we go to meet the strife,
 We will not fear nor fly;
We love the holy warrior's life,
 His death we hope to die.
We slumber not, that charge in view,
 "Toil on while toil ye may,
Then night shall be no night to you,
 Ye children of the day!"

2 Guard us waking, guard us sleeping,
    And, when we die,
May we in Thy mighty keeping
    All peaceful lie:
When the heav'nly call shall wake us,
Do not Thou our God forsake us,
But to reign in glory take us
    With Thee on high.

GOD IN NATURE.

42. J. KEBLE.   LIBER. C.M.D.   L. SPOHR.

Joyously.

1. There is a book, who runs may read, Which heav'n-ly truth im-parts;
And all the lore its schol-ars need, Pure eyes and Chris-tian hearts.
The works of God, a-bove, be-low, With-in us and a-round,
Are pag-es in that book, to show How God him-self is found. A-MEN.

2 The glorious sky, embracing all,
   Is like the Maker's love,
Wherewith encompassed, great and small
   In peace and order move.
Thou who hast given us eyes to see
   And love this sight so fair,
Give us a heart to find out Thee,
   And read Thee everywhere! AMEN.

GOD IN NATURE.

43. J. G. WHITTIER.   HERZOG. C. M. D.

1. The harp at Nature's advent strung Has never ceased to play;
The song the stars of morning sung Has never died away.
And prayer is made, and praise is given, By all things near and far:
The ocean looketh up to heav'n And mirrors ev'ry star.

2 The green earth sends her incense up
From many a mountain shrine;
From folded leaf and dewy cup
She pours her sacred wine.
The blue sky is the temple's arch;
Its transept, earth, and air;
The music of its starry march
The chorus of a prayer.

44. GOLDEN DAYS. 8s & 7s. D.

Mrs. E. H. Leland.
Music composed for this Hymnal by E. H. Bailey.

1. The days are glid-ing swift-ly by, The days so bright and gold-en;
   In leaf and flow'r the sum-mer writes Her po-em sweet and old-en.
2. The earth is warm with life and joy, The air is full of splen-dor;
   And un-to all the south wind brings Her mes-sage sweet and ten-der.

CHORUS.
The gold-en days! the long bright days! The glad-dest of the year!
The green grass springs, the wild bird sings,— The sum-mer time is here!

3 Oh, Giver of these summer hours,
   All nature sings Thy praises,
   From mountain peak to where the flow'r
   Its lowly bloom upraises!
     The golden days, etc.

4 And at Thy feet we too would sing,
   With all Thy creatures living,
   A song of mirth, a song of joy,
   A song of glad thanksgiving.
     The golden days, etc.

GOD IN NATURE.

45. W. C. Gannett.   LILIUM. 7s & 6s. D.   Rev. J. B. Dykes.

1. He hides with-in the lil-y A strong and ten-der care,
That wins the earth-born at-oms To glo-ry of the air.
He weaves the shin-ing gar-ments Un-ceas-ing-ly and still,
A-long the qui-et wa-ters, In nich-es of the hill.

2 We linger at the vigil
  With him who bent the knee
To watch the old-time lilies
  In distant Galilee;
And still the worship deepens
  And quickens into new,
As brightening down the ages
  God's secret thrilleth through.

3 O Toiler of the Lily!
  Thy touch is in the Man;
No leaf that dawns to petal
  But hints the angel-plan.
The flower-horizons open;
  The blossom vaster shows;
We hear Thy wide worlds echo,—
  "See how the lily grows!"

GOD IN NATURE.

46. Bp. Cotton.   PRAISE. L. M. D.   John Adcock.

1. We thank Thee, Lord, for this fair earth, The glit-t'ring sky, the sil-ver sea; For all their beau-ty, all their worth, Their light and glo-ry, come from Thee. Thine are the flow'rs that clothe the ground, The trees that weave their arms a-bove, The hills that gird our dwell-ings round, As Thou dost gird Thine own with love.

2 Yet teach us still how far more fair,
  Thou glorious Father, in Thy sight,
Is one pure deed, one holy prayer,
  One heart that owns Thy Spirit's might.
So while we gaze with thoughtful eye
  On all the gifts Thy love has given,
Help us in Thee to live and die,
  By Thee to rise from earth to heaven.

GOD IN NATURE.

47. F. S. Pierpont.   **VERONA.** 7s, 6 lines.   Italian.

2 For the wonder of each hour
  Of the day and of the night,
  Hill and vale, and tree and flower,
  Sun and moon, and stars of light,—
  Lord of all, to Thee we raise
  This our grateful psalm of praise.

GOD IN NATURE.

48. Sir J. Bowring.   SOPHIA. 8s & 7s.   Italian Melody.

1. God is love! His mercy bright-ens All the path in which we rove;
   Bliss He wakes, and woe He light-ens: God is wis-dom, God is love.
2. Chance and change are bus-y ev-er; Man de-cays, and a-ges move;
   But His mer-cy wan-eth nev-er: God is wis-dom, God is love.

3 E'en the hour that darkest seemeth
   Will His changeless goodness prove;
   From the gloom His brightness streameth:
   God is wisdom, God is love.

4 He with earthly cares entwineth
   Hope and comfort from above;
   Everywhere His glory shineth:
   God is wisdom, God is love.

49. Isaac Watts.   SHARON. C.M.   T. Wallhead.

1. I sing the might-y pow'r of God, That made the moun-tains rise;
   That spread the flow-ing seas a-broad, And built the lof-ty skies.
2. I sing the wis-dom that or-dain'd The sun to rule the day:
   The moon shines full at His com-mand, And all the stars o-bey.

3 I sing the goodness of the Lord,
   That fill'd the earth with food:
   He form'd the creatures with His word,
   And then pronounced them good.

4 There's not a plant or flow'r below
   But makes His glories known;
   And clouds arise, and tempests blow,
   By order from His throne.

GOD IN NATURE.

50.   **CREATION.** 7s. D.   John Hullah.

1. Ev-'ry gen-tle gale that blows, Ev-'ry lit-tle stream that flows
Thro' the green and flow'r-y vale, Ev-'ry flow'r that scents the gale,
Ev-'ry soft re-fresh-ing show'r Sent up-on the droop-ing flow'r,
Ev-'ry tem-pest rush-ing by, Says to man that God is nigh. A-MEN.

2 Lofty hills with forests crowned,
Deserts where no tree is found,
Rivers from the mountain's source
Winding on their fruitful course,
Ocean with its mighty waves,
Rocks and sands, and pearly caves,
All that in the ocean dwell
Unto us His goodness tell.

3 Every little creeping thing,
Every insect on the wing,
Every bird that warbling flies
Freely through his native skies,
Beasts that far from man abide,
Those that gambol by his side,
Cattle on a thousand hills,
Say that God creation fills. AMEN.

GOD IN NATURE.

51. J. Conder.   **DAY UNTO DAY.** 7s & 6s. D.   John Adcock.

1. The heav'ns declare His glory; Their Maker's skill the skies;
Each day repeats the story, And night to night replies.
Their silent proclamation Throughout the earth is heard,—
The record of creation, The page of Nature's word.

2 There, from his bright pavilion,
   Like Eastern bridegroom clad,
Hailed by earth's thousand million,
   The sun sets forth: right glad,
His glorious race commencing,
   The mighty giant seems;
Through the vast round dispensing
   His all-pervading beams.

3 So pure, so soul-restoring,
   Is Truth's diviner ray;
A brighter radiance pouring
   Than all the pomp of day:
The wand'rer surely guiding,
   It makes the simple wise;
And evermore abiding,
   Unfailing joy supplies.

GOD IN NATURE.

52. J. S BLACKIE. **ANGELS HOLY.** P. M. HENRY FARMER.

1. An-gels ho-ly, High and low-ly, Sing the prais-es of the Lord!
2. Sun and moon bright, Night and noon-light, Star-ry tem-ples a-zure floor'd,
3. O-ceans hoar-y Tell His glo-ry; Cliffs where tumbling seas have roar'd;

Earth and sky, all liv-ing Na-ture, Man, the stamp of
Cloud and rain and wild wind's mad-ness, Sons of God that
Pulse of wa-ter, blithe-ly beat-ing, Wave ad-vanc-ing,

thy Cre-a-tor,—Praise ye, praise ye God the Lord!
shout for gladness,—Praise ye, praise ye God the Lord!
wave re-treat-ing,—Praise ye, praise ye God the Lord!

4 Rocks and highland,
  Wood and island,
Crag where eagle's pride hath soar'd,
Mighty mountains purple-breasted,
Peaks cloud-cleaving, snowy-crested,—
Praise ye, praise ye God the Lord!

5 Praise Him ever,
  Bounteous Giver!
Praise Him, Father, Friend, and Lord!
Each glad soul its free course winging,
Each glad voice its free song singing,—
Praise ye, praise ye God the Lord!

53. **LAW OF BEAUTY.** P. M. J. BERTHOLD.

1. "What is the law of thy beau-ty?" I ask'd of the op'n-ing rose,—

GOD IN NATURE.

The queen of the flow'rs of the gar - den, The copse, the field, the close:
And in o - dors sweet it said to me, "Do thy du-ty, and thou shalt see!"

2 "What is the law of thy beauty?"
   I ask'd of the drop of dew
   That hung in the plume of the daisy
   That leaned o'er violets blue:
   And in crystal tho'ts it said to me,
   "Do thy duty, and thou shalt see!"

3 "What is the law of thy beauty?"
   I ask'd of the lichen pale
   That grew like a dream of the spring-time
   Through winter's storm and hail:
   And its tiny shields replied to me,
   "Do thy duty, and thou shalt see!"

54.   FLORA. S. M.
Music composed for this Hymnal by T. W. Surette.

1. The freshly-blooming flow'rs   To Thee sweet off'rings bear,   And cheerful birds in shad-y bow'rs Sing forth Thy ten-der care,— Sing forth Thy ten-der care.
2. The fields on ev'-ry side,   The trees on ev'-ry hill,   The glorious sun, the roll-ing tide, Pro-claim Thy won-ders still,— Pro-claim Thy won-ders still.

3 But trees and fields and skies
   Still praise a God unknown;
   For gratitude and love can rise
   ||: From living hearts alone. :||

4 These living hearts of ours
   Thy holy name would bless;
   The blossoms of all Nature's flowers
   ||: Would please our Father less. :||

2 When day, with farewell beam, delays
Among the opening clouds of even,
And we can almost think we gaze
Through golden vistas into heaven,—
Those hues, that make the sun's decline
So soft, so radiant, Lord, are Thine.

3 When youthful Spring around us breathes,
Thy spirit warms her fragrant sigh;
And every flower the summer wreathes
Is born beneath Thy kindling eye:
Where'er we turn, Thy glories shine,
And all things fair and bright are Thine.

GOD IN NATURE.

56. A. LAIGHTON.   BELMONT. C. M.   S. WEBBE.

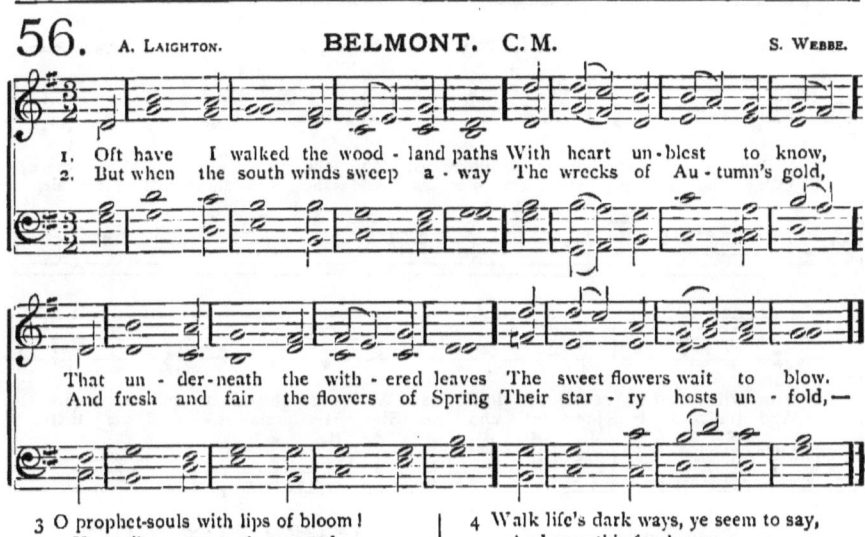

1. Oft have I walked the wood-land paths With heart un-blest to know,
That un-der-neath the with-ered leaves The sweet flowers wait to blow.
2. But when the south winds sweep a-way The wrecks of Au-tumn's gold,
And fresh and fair the flowers of Spring Their star-ry hosts un-fold,—

3 O prophet-souls with lips of bloom!
   Your silence, more than speech,
Fills all the woody aisles, like songs
   That faith and duty teach.

4 Walk life's dark ways, ye seem to say,
   And ever this foreknow,—
That, where man sees but withered leaves,
   God sees the sweet flowers grow!

57.   NATURE'S SONG. C. M.   Rev. J. B. DYKES.

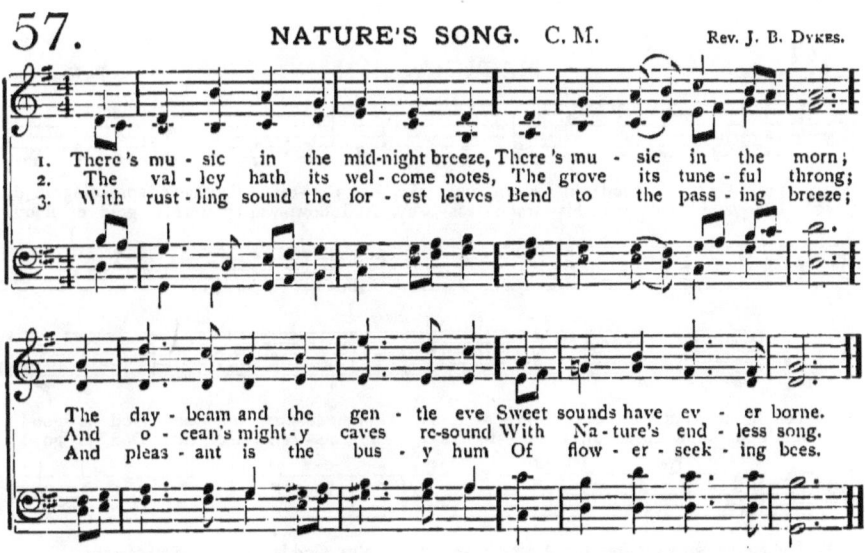

1. There's mu-sic in the mid-night breeze, There's mu-sic in the morn;
The day-beam and the gen-tle eve Sweet sounds have ev-er borne.
2. The val-ley hath its wel-come notes, The grove its tune-ful throng;
And o-cean's might-y caves re-sound With Na-ture's end-less song.
3. With rust-ling sound the for-est leaves Bend to the pass-ing breeze;
And pleas-ant is the bus-y hum Of flow-er-seek-ing bees.

4 The heart, too, has its melodies,—
   A consecrated spring
From which mysterious voices flow,
   And songs of gladness ring.

5 Why Nature's music, but that man
   May join the myriad throng
Of all her glorious works in one
   Harmonious burst of song?

GOD IN NATURE.

58. Rev. C. T. Brooks.   **CLINTON.** 8s & 7s.   Arthur Page.

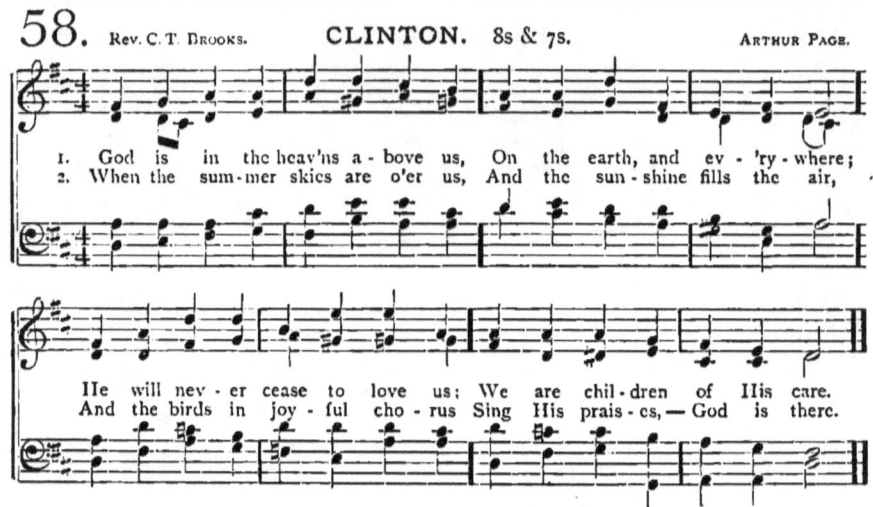

1. God is in the heav'ns a-bove us, On the earth, and ev-'ry-where;
   He will nev-er cease to love us: We are chil-dren of His care.
2. When the sum-mer skies are o'er us, And the sun-shine fills the air,
   And the birds in joy-ful cho-rus Sing His prais-es,— God is there.

3 When the stars in winter glisten,
   And the trees are brown and bare,
  God, our Father, then will listen
   To the little snow-birds' prayer.

4 Let us love Him and adore Him
   Who has made this world so fair!
  Singing, as we walk before Him,
   God is with us everywhere!

59.   **NATURA.** L. M.   C. E. Willing.

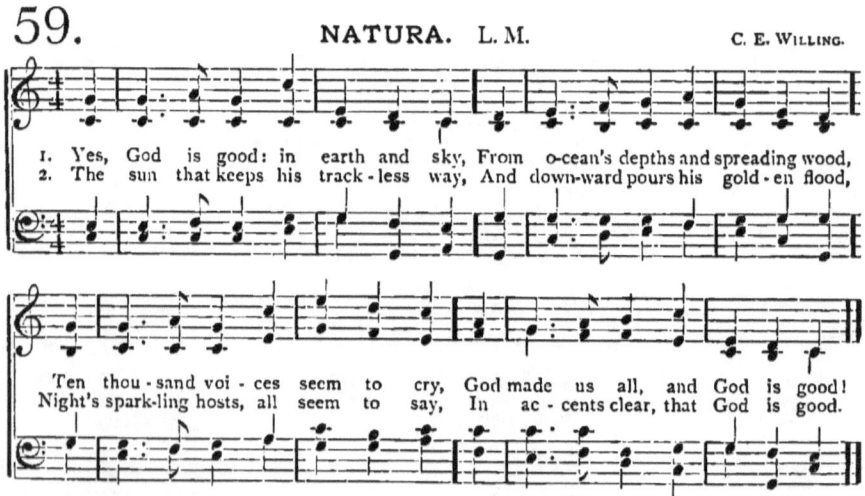

1. Yes, God is good: in earth and sky, From o-cean's depths and spreading wood,
   Ten thou-sand voi-ces seem to cry, God made us all, and God is good!
2. The sun that keeps his track-less way, And down-ward pours his gold-en flood,
   Night's spark-ling hosts, all seem to say, In ac-cents clear, that God is good.

3 The merry birds prolong the strain,
   Their song with ev'ry spring renewed;
  And balmy air, and falling rain,
   Each softly whispers, God is good!

4 Yes, God is good, all Nature says,
   By God's own hand with speech endued;
  And man, in louder notes of praise,
   Should sing for joy that God is good.

2 Health, peace, and joy attend us,
  Kind friends are ever near;
O Father, Thou dost send us
  Unnumbered blessings here!
And though we, in our blindness,
  Enjoy, but disobey,
Yet still, Thou, in Thy kindness,
  Tak'st not Thy gifts away.

3 Here, then, in childhood's morning,
  Our hymns to Thee we raise;
Thy love, our lives adorning,
  Shall fill our hearts with praise.
Thy will, henceforth, forever
  Shall be our only guide;
From duty's path we 'd never,
  Oh, never, turn aside! AMEN.

RELIGION OF CHILDHOOD.

61. James D. Burns.   **ANTWERP.** C. M. D.   Hollandish Air.

1. As helpless as a child who clings Fast to his father's arm,
And casts his weakness on the strength That keeps him safe from harm,—
So I, my Father, cling to Thee, And ev'ry passing hour
Would link my earthly feebleness To Thine almighty pow'r. A-MEN.

2 As trustful as a child who looks
   Up in his mother's face,
And all his little griefs and fears
   Forgets in her embrace,—
So unto Thee, O Lord, I look,
   And in Thy face divine
Can read the love that will sustain
   As weak a faith as mine.

3 As loving as a child who sits
   Close by his parent's knee,
And knows no want while it can have
   That sweet society,—
So, sitting at Thy feet, my heart
   Would all its love outpour,
And pray that Thou wouldst teach me, Lord,
   To love Thee more and more. AMEN.

RELIGION OF CHILDHOOD.

62. J. H. Gurney. HOLYROOD. S.M. Sir R. Stewart.

1. Fair waved the gold-en corn In Ca-naan's pleas-ant land. When full of joy some shi-ning morn Went forth the reap-er band. A-MEN.
2. To God so good and great Their cheer-ful thanks they pour; Then car-ry to His tem-ple-gate The choic-est of their store. A-MEN.

3 Like Israel, Lord, we give
 Our earliest fruits to Thee;
And pray that, long as we shall live,
 We may Thy children be.

4 In wisdom let us grow,
 As years and strength are given,
That we may serve Thee here below,
 And join Thy saints in heaven. AMEN.

63. GLADSOME HYMN. 7s. Rev. J. B. Dykes.

1. God of mer-cy and of love, Lis-ten from Thy Heav'n a-bove, While to Thee my voice I raise, In a glad-some hymn of praise. A-MEN.

2 Father, keep me all day long
 From all hurtful things and wrong;
Make me an obedient child,
Make me loving, gentle, mild.

3 Make me, Lord, in work and play,
 Thine more truly every day;
And when Thou at last shalt come,
Take me to Thy Heavenly Home. AMEN.

66. SWEETEST NAME. P.M.

Arthur Page.

1. The sweet-est name in heav'n a-bove,
   Children sing, children sing!
   Our Heav'n-ly Fa-ther, God of love,
   Children sing to-day!
   The Friend whose ev-er-watch-ful care
   Will guard our feet from ev'-ry snare,
   Who loves to hear our ear-nest pray'r,—
   Chil-dren sing to-day!

2 With those whose trials now are o'er,
   Children sing, children sing!
With saints on yonder radiant shore,
   Children sing to-day!
With martyrs in the heav'nly land,
That round His throne in glory stand,
With all the shining angel band,—
   Children sing to-day!

RELIGION OF CHILDHOOD.

67.   SHELTERED VALE. C. M. 6 lines.   German.

1. O lit-tle birds that all day long Car-ol in ev'-ry tree,
What is the se-cret of your song, The mean-ing of your glee?
You are so ve-ry, ve-ry glad,— How lov-ing God must be!

2 Dear flowers that blossom round my feet,
   It fills my heart to see
Your smiling faces, when you meet
   God's wind upon the lea;
You seem to laugh for happiness,—
   How loving God must be!

3 And all day long our hearts rejoice,—
   God cares for you and me;
We are but children, yet our voice
   May praise Him merrily;
And we can sing like all the birds,—
   How loving God must be!

68.   Rev. BROOKE HERFORD.   FRANCONIA. P. M.   Bristol Tune Book.

1. Lead us, Heav'nly Fa-ther, Lead us, Shep-herd kind; We are on-ly
2. Lead us, Heav'nly Fa-ther, In our op'n-ing way; Lead us in the

RELIGION OF CHILDHOOD.

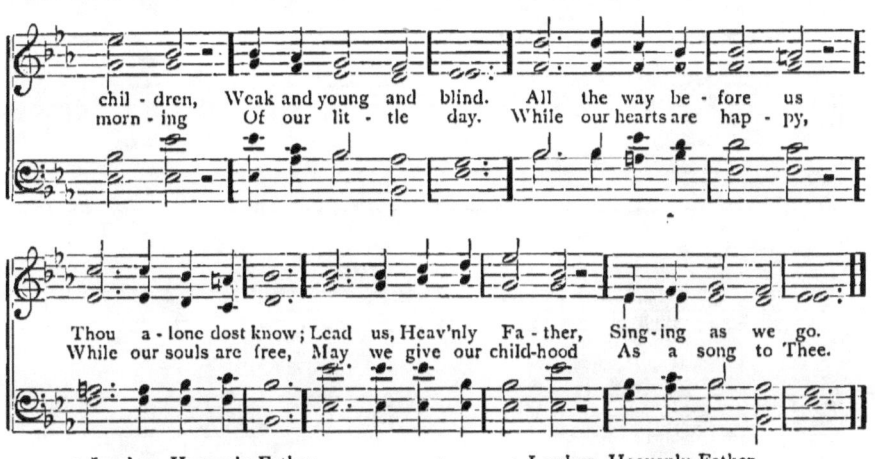

3 Lead us, Heavenly Father,
  As the way grows long;
  Be our strong salvation,
  Be our joyous song.
  Gladdened by Thy mercies,
  Chastened by Thy rod,
  May we walk thro' all things
  Humbly with our God.

4 Lead us, Heavenly Father,
  By Thy voices clear,
  Through the prophets holy,
  Through the Saviour dear, —
  He who took the children
  In his arm of love:
  May we all be gathered
  In his home above!

69. JOHN D. LONG.   HINGHAM. C. M.   WEBER.

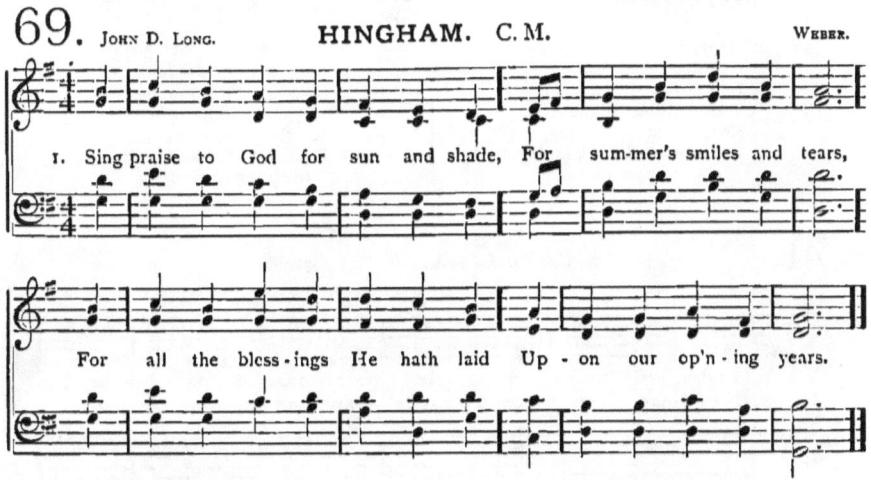

2 Sing to each other truer love,
  Affection's kindly glow;
  The tenderness of God above
  In human hearts below.

3 E'en as the dews at evening fall, —
  So, smiling on the day,
  May God at eve upon us all
  His benediction lay.

RELIGION OF CHILDHOOD.

70. W. H Groser. **SUNNY DAYS.** P. M. Arr. by C. Darnton.

1. Sun-ny days of child-hood! Beau-ti-ful ye seem;
Fair as spring-tide flow-ers, Bright as sum-mer's beam.
Days with joy o'er-flow-ing, Care nor sad-ness know-ing, Must ye pass a-way?

2 Happy days of childhood!
Swiftly moving on;
Into manhood changing,
Ye will soon be gone.
Like a streamlet flowing,
Pause nor stillness knowing,
Thus ye pass away.

3 Precious days of childhood!
Days of promise fair!
If bedew'd with wisdom,
Rich the fruits ye bear.
Jesus' footsteps keeping,
Blest shall be our reaping
In life's harvest day.

71. **CAROLINA.** 8.7.8.7.4.7.

Hymns of the Spirit. Music composed for this Hymnal by Rev. E. C. L. Browne.

1. Fa-ther, hear the pray'r we of-fer! Not for ease that pray'r shall be;
2. Not for - ev - er in green pas-tures Do we ask our way to be;

RELIGION OF CHILDHOOD.

But for strength that we may ev-er Live our lives cou-rage-ous-ly.
But the steep and rug-ged path-way May we tread re-joic-ing-ly.

Heav'n-ly Fa-ther, Heav'n-ly Fa-ther, Hear the pray'r we of-fer now!

3 Not forever by still waters
  Would we idly quiet stay;
  But would smite the living fountains
  From the rocks along our way.
    Heavn'ly Father, etc.

4 Be our strength in hours of weakness;
  In our wand'rings be our guide;
  Through endeavor, failure, danger,
  Father, be Thou at our side!
    Heav'nly Father, etc.

72. PETITION. 7.7.7.6.   T. Morley.

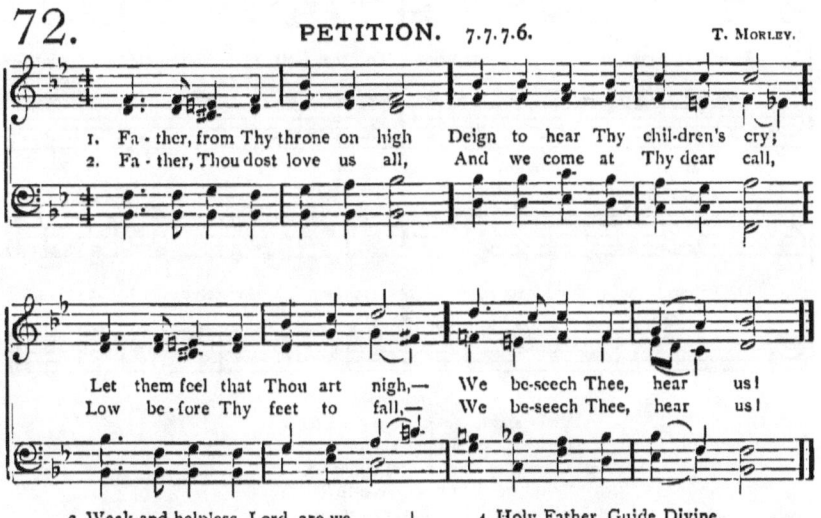

1. Fa-ther, from Thy throne on high Deign to hear Thy chil-dren's cry;
2. Fa-ther, Thou dost love us all, And we come at Thy dear call,

Let them feel that Thou art nigh,— We be-seech Thee, hear us!
Low be-fore Thy feet to fall,— We be-seech Thee, hear us!

3 Weak and helpless, Lord, are we,
  Yet Thy love is all our plea;
  Suffer us to come to Thee,—
    We beseech Thee, hear us!

4 Holy Father, Guide Divine,
  Let Thy Light forever shine;
  Leave us not, for we are Thine,—
    We beseech Thee, hear us!

2 Vows and longings, hopes and fears,
Broken-hearted sighs and tears,
Dreams of what we yet might be,
Could we cling more close to Thee;
All that childlike love can render
Of devotion true and tender, —
On Thine altar laid we leave them:
O receive them, Lord! receive them! AMEN.

RELIGION OF CHILDHOOD.

74. CHILDHOOD'S INNOCENCE. C. M. D.

Thomas Gray, Jr. A. Randegger.

1. We come in childhood's innocence, We come as children free:
We offer up, O God, our hearts In trusting love to Thee.
Well may we think with sacred joy Of Thy bright courts above!
Well may the grateful child rejoice In such a Father's love!

2 We come not as the mighty come;
  Not as the proud we bow;
  But as the pure in heart should find,
  Seek we thine altar now.
  In joy we wake, in peace we sleep,
  Safe from all dread alarms;
  Not folded in an angel's wings,
  But in a Father's arms.

RELIGION OF CHILDHOOD.

75.   PAGE. P. M.   ARTHUR PAGE.

1. Hark! round the God of love Angels are singing; Saints at Thy feet above Their crowns are flinging. And may Thy children dare Hope for acceptance there, Our simple praise and pray'r To Thy throne bringing?

2 Not a poor sparrow falls
   But Thou art near it;
When the young raven calls,
   Thou, Lord, dost hear it.
Flowers, birds, and insects share
Hourly Thy guardian care:
Wilt Thou bid us despair?
   Lord, can we fear it?

3 Lord, then Thy mercy send
   On all before Thee;
Children and children's friend
   Bless, we implore Thee:
Lead us from grace to grace,
On through our earthly race,
Till all before Thy face
   Meet to adore Thee.

76.   CHILDREN'S LITANY. 7.7.7.6.
THOMAS B. POLLOCK.   H. WOODS.

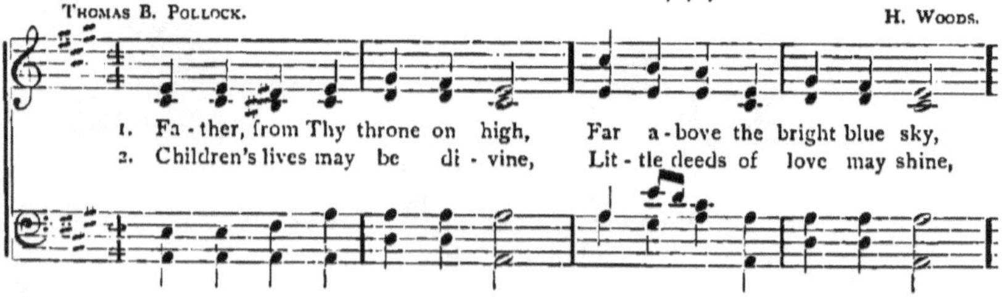

1. Father, from Thy throne on high, Far above the bright blue sky,
2. Children's lives may be divine, Little deeds of love may shine,

RELIGION OF CHILDHOOD.

Look on us with lov-ing eye,— Hear us, O our Fa-ther!
Youthful hearts be whol-ly Thine,— Hear us, O our Fa-ther!

3 Be Thou with us every day,
In our work and in our play,
When we learn and when we pray,—
Hear us, O our Father!

4 Make us brave, without a fear;
Make us happy, full of cheer,
Sure that Thou art always near,—
Hear us, O our Father!

77. MARY E. SHELLY.   ST. RAPHAEL. 8.7.8.7.4.7.   E. J. HOPKINS.

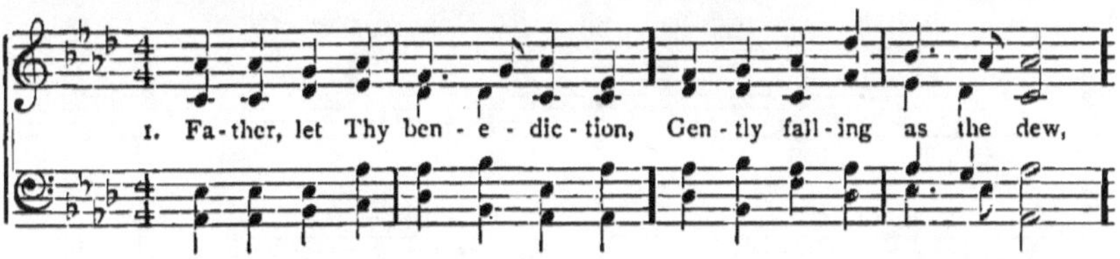

1. Fa-ther, let Thy ben-e-dic-tion, Gen-tly fall-ing as the dew,
And Thy ev-er-gra-cious pres-ence, Bless us all our jour-ney through!
May we ev-er keep the end of life in view! A-MEN.

After last verse.

2 Young in years, we need the wisdom
Which can only come from Thee;
In the morn of our existence
Let us Thy salvation see!
Pure in spirit,
Then shall we Thy children be.

3 When temptation shall assail us,
When we falter by the way,
Let Thine arm of strength defend us,—
Father, hear us when we pray!
Thou art mighty;
Be Thou, then, our rock and stay! AMEN.

2 God make my life a little flower
   That giveth joy to all;
   Content to bloom in native bower,
   Although its place be small!
      O Father, help Thy children! etc.

3 God make my life a little staff
   Whereon the weak may rest;
   That so what health and strength I have
   May serve my neighbors best!
      O Father, help Thy children! etc.

PROCESSIONAL.

79. ONWARD, CHRISTIAN SOLDIERS. 6s & 5s, 12 lines.

Rev. S. Baring-Gould.   Sir Arthur S. Sullivan.

2 Like a mighty army
   Moves the Church of God :
Brothers, we are treading
   Where the saints have trod ;
May we not divided
   But united be ;
One in faith and duty,
   One in charity.
      Onward, Christian soldiers, etc.

3 Onward, then, ye people,
   Join our happy throng,
Blend with ours your voices
   In triumphant song !
Glory, praise, and honor,
   Unto God, our King, —
This, through countless ages,
   Men and angels sing.
      Onward, Christian soldiers, etc.   Amen.

PROCESSIONAL.

83. FESTIVAL. 7s & 6s.

1. Forth to the fight, ye faithful, Mighty in God's own might,
Stemming the tide of battle, Routing the hosts of night!
Lift ye the red cross banner, Wield ye the victor's sword,
Raise ye the Christian's war-cry,— "We're soldiers of the Lord!" AMEN.

2. Arm ye against the battle, Strive ye, and watch, and pray!
Peace shall succeed the warfare, Night shall be changed to day.

3 Fear not the din of battle,
   Follow where Christ has trod;
   Conquer the hosts of darkness
   Strong in the might of God!
   Lift ye, etc.

4 Fight, for the Lord is o'er you,
   Fight, for He bids you fight;
   There where the fray is thickest
   Close with the hosts of night!
   Lift ye, etc.

PROCESSIONAL.

84. H. Alford.   STANDARD. 6s & 5s. 12 lines.   H. Smart.

1. Forward! be our watchword, Steps and voi-ces joined; Seek the things be-fore us,
Not a look be-hind! Burns the fier-y pil-lar At our ar-my's head:
Who shall dream of shrink-ing, By our Cap-tain led? Forward, out of er-ror,
Leave be-hind the night! Forward thro' the dark-ness, For-ward in-to light! A-MEN.

After last verse.

2 Far o'er yon horizon
  Rise the city towers,
Where our God abideth:
  That fair home is ours.
Flash the streets with jasper;
  Shine the gates with gold;
Flows the gladdening river,
  Shedding joys untold.
Thither, onward thither,
  In the Spirit's might,
Pilgrims, homeward going,
  Forward into light! AMEN.

PROCESSIONAL.

85. CHILDREN'S MARCH. P.M.

Rev. H. F. Sheppard. Rev. H. F. Sheppard.

1. Oh, val-iant lit-tle sol-diers, Why march you thus a-long,
2. Oh, val-iant lit-tle sol-diers, But you are weak and frail!
3. Oh, val-iant lit-tle sol-diers, Take me a-long with you;

And lift your child-ish voic-es In loud and war-like song?
The way is long, the foe is strong, And dan-gers sore as-sail;
You serve the Lord and trust His word,— I'll serve and trust Him too.

Whose ban-ner do you bear a-loft,— A cross as red as flame?
Un-known temp-ta-tions hov-er near, Sin lurks on ev'-ry hand;
I too will bear His ban-ner fair; I too will con-quer sin:

PROCESSIONAL.

MINISTRY OF JESUS.

86. PILGRIMAGE. 7.6.7.6.7.6.7.3. T. L. Selby.

1. The world looks ve-ry beau-ti-ful And full of joy to me;
   The sun shines out in glo-ry On ev'-ry thing I see;
   I know I shall be hap-py While in the world I stay,
   For I will fol-low Je-sus — All the way.

2. I'm but a youth-ful pil-grim; My jour-ney's just be-gun;
   They say I'll meet with sor-row Be-fore my jour-ney's done.
   The world is full of trou-ble, And tri-als, too, they say;
   But I will fol-low Je-sus — All the way.

3 Then, like a youthful pilgrim,
  Whatever I may meet,
  I'll take it — joy or sorrow —
  And lay it at God's feet.
  He'll comfort me in trouble,
  He'll wipe my tears away;
  With joy I'll follow Jesus —
  All the way.

4 Then trials cannot vex me,
  And pain I need not fear;
  For when I follow Jesus,
  Grief cannot come too near.
  Not even death can harm me,
  When death I meet one day;
  To heaven I'll follow Jesus —
  All the way.

87. Rev. S. Longfellow. CLARABELLA. C.M.

1. Beneath the shadow of the cross, As earthly hopes remove, His new commandment Jesus gives,—His blessed word of love.

2 O bond of union, strong and deep!
O bond of perfect peace!
Not even the lifted cross can harm,
If we but hold to this.

3 Then, Jesus, be thy spirit ours;
And swift our feet shall move
To deeds of pure self-sacrifice,
And the sweet tasks of love.

88. Rev. J. M. Neale. ART THOU WEARY? P.M. Arr. by W. H. Monk.

1. Art thou weary? art thou languid? Art thou sore distress'd?
2. Hath he marks to lead me to him, If he be my guide?
3. Is there diadem, as monarch, That his brow adorns?

"Come to me," saith one; "and coming, Be at rest!"
"In his feet and hands are wound-prints, And his side!"
"Yes! a crown in very surety, But of thorns!" A-MEN.

After last verse.

4 If I find him, if I follow,
What his guerdon here?
"Many a sorrow, many a labor,
Many a tear."

5 If I still hold closely to him,
What hath he at last?
"Sorrow vanquish'd, labor ended,
Jordan passed."

6 If I ask him to receive me,
Will he say me nay?
"Not till earth and not till heaven
Pass away."

7 Finding, following, keeping, struggling,
Is he sure to bless?
"Saints, apostles, prophets, martyrs,
Answer, Yes!" AMEN.

MINISTRY OF JESUS.

89. J. G. Whittier. **WHITTIER. C. M. D.** Dr. Croft.

1. He cometh not a king to reign,—The world's long hope is dim;
The weary cent-'ries watch in vain The clouds of heav'n for him.
But warm, sweet, tender, even yet A present help is he;
And faith has still its Ol-i-vet, And love its Gal-i-lee.

2 The healing of his seamless dress
  Is by our beds of pain;
We touch him in life's throng and press,
  And we are whole again.
O Friend and Teacher of us all!
  Whate'er our name or sign,
Thy words like heavenly music fall,
  And draw our lives to thine.

MINISTRY OF JESUS.

90. ST. CATHERINE. 8s & 7s.
Moderate.

1. Ev - er would we fain be read - ing, In the an - cient ho - ly Book,
2. How, when children came, he blessed them, Suffered no man to re - prove;

Of the Saviour's gen - tle pleading,— Truth in ev' - ry word and look:
Took them in his arms, and pressed them To his heart with words of love:

3 How to all the sick and tearful
   Help was ever gladly shown;
   How he sought the poor and fearful,
   Called them brothers, and his own.

4 Father, as we journey onward,
   Make us Christlike day by day;
   Daily knowing Jesus better,
   As the Life, the Truth, the Way!

91. MELCOMBE. L.M.
JOHN D. LONG.   S. WEBBE.

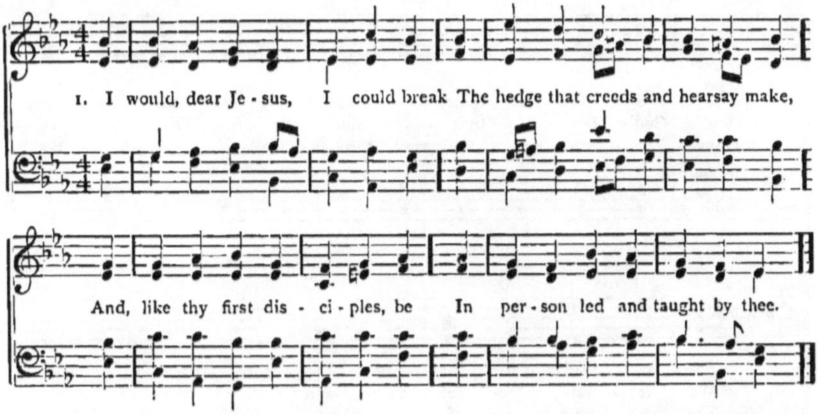

1. I would, dear Je - sus, I could break The hedge that creeds and hearsay make,

And, like thy first dis - ci - ples, be In per - son led and taught by thee.

2 I read thy words,— they are so sweet;
   I seek the footprints of thy feet;
   But men so mystify the trace,
   I long to see thee face to face.

3 Wouldst thou not let me, at thy side,
   In thee, in thee so sure, confide?
   Like John, upon thy breast recline,
   And feel thy heart make mine divine?

MINISTRY OF JESUS.

MINISTRY OF JESUS.

93. BUFFINGTON. C.M.
J. G. Whittier.   Composed for this Hymnal by E. H. Bailey.

1. O Love! O Life! our faith and sight Thy presence maketh one.
As thro' trans-fig-ured clouds of white We trace the noon-day sun,—
2. So to our mortal eyes subdued, Flesh-veil'd, but not conceal'd,
We know in thee the fatherhood And heart of God reveal'd.

3 We faintly hear, we dimly see,
  In diff'ring phrase we pray;
But, dim or clear, we own in thee
  The Light, the Truth, the Way.

4 Our Friend, our Brother, and our Guide,
  What may thy service be?—
Nor name, nor form, nor ritual pride,
  But simply following thee.

94. BOWRING. 8s & 7s.
Sir John Bowring.   Dr. Boyce.

1. In the cross of Christ I glory, Tow'ring o'er the wrecks of time;
All the light of sacred story Gathers round its head sublime.
2. When the woes of life o'ertake me, Hopes deceive, and fears annoy,
Never shall the cross forsake me; Lo, it glows with peace and joy!

3 When the sun of bliss is beaming
  Light and love upon my way,
From the cross the radiance streaming
  Adds more lustre to the day.

4 Bane and blessing, pain and pleasure,
  By the cross are sanctified;
Peace is there that knows no measure,
  Joys that through all time abide.

MINISTRY OF JESUS.

95. FOLLOW ME. P. M. German.

1. "Follow me," the Master said: We will follow Jesus;
By his word and spirit led, We will follow Jesus.
In our daily round of care, As we raise to God our prayer,
With the cross which we must bear, We will follow Jesus.

2 Ever keep the end in view, —
    We will follow Jesus;
All his promises are true, —
    We will follow Jesus;
When this earthly course is run,
And the Master says, "Well done,"
Life eternal we have won!
    We will follow Jesus.

MINISTRY OF JESUS.

Hail the sign of Jesus, Chasing far our fear!
Where-so-e'er it goeth Should Christ's soldiers be.
On, then, Christian soldiers! On to victory!

CHORUS.

Hail the Cross of Jesus! Lift it up on high!

Unison.

Hail the mighty signal Pointing to the sky!

MINISTRY OF JESUS.

98. Charlotte Elliott.   MARGARET. P. M.   Rev. T. R. Matthews.

1. Heav'n's arch-es rang when the an-gels sang, Pro-claim-ing thy high de-gree; But in low-ly birth didst thou come to earth, And in great hu-mil-i-ty. Oh, come to my heart, dear Je-sus! There is room in my heart for thee! A-MEN.

2 The foxes found rest, and the bird had its nest
　In the shade of the cedar-tree;
But thy couch was the sod, O thou Son of God,
　In the desert of Galilee.
　　　Oh, come to my heart, dear Jesus!
　　　There is room in my heart for thee!

3 Thou camest to men with the living word
　That should set all people free;
But with mocking scorn, and with crown of thorn,
　They bore thee to Calvary.
　　　Oh, come to my heart, dear Jesus!
　　　There is room in my heart for thee! AMEN.

MINISTRY OF JESUS.

99. T. Goadby. **INVITATION.** P. M. Henry Farmer.

1. When the day of life is dawning, Come, come to me;
In the heart's fresh, early morning, Come, come to me;
While thine eye with hope is beaming, While thy soul of heav'n is dreaming,
And its light is round thee streaming, Come, come to me, to me.

2 Ere sin's tainted touch defile thee,
   Come, come to me;
Ere the world's false joys beguile thee,
   Come, come to me;
While the dew of youth is on thee,
And no heavy cares upon thee,
Ere the tempter's power has won thee,
   Come, come to me.

3 When the day of life is dawning,
   Come, come to me;
In the heart's fresh, early morning,
   Come, come to me;
Ere earth's sickly pleasure palleth,
Ere one shade of sorrow falleth,
List to that sweet voice which calleth,
   Come, come to me.

MINISTRY OF JESUS.

100. PEACE. 8.8.8.3.

1. Fierce rag'd the tempest o'er the deep; Watch did the tired disciples keep;
The Master lay in dreamless sleep, Calm and still.
2. "Save, Lord! we perish!" was their cry; "Oh, save us in our agony!"
Above the storm the word rose high: "Peace! be still!"

3 The wild winds hush'd; the angry deep
Sank, like a little child, to sleep;
The sullen billows ceased to leap;—
All was still!

4 So, Father, when we drift from shore,
And all our life is clouded o'er,
Bid Passion's fierce and angry roar—
"Peace! be still!"

101. HEILSBERG. 7s.
C. WESLEY.   J F. CHRISTMANN.

1. God of Jesus, hear me now Take the meek disciple's vow!
Thou, so good, so true, so kind, Fill me with the Saviour's mind!
2. Plant, and root, and fix in me Trust, as of a child, in Thee;
Settled peace I then shall find, Like the Saviour's quiet mind.
3. I shall suffer and fulfil All my Father's gracious will;
Be in ev'ry lot resign'd, Like the Saviour's patient mind.

4 When his faith is rooted here,
Perfect love shall cast out fear;
Fear doth servile spirits bind,
Not the Saviour's noble mind.

5 Lowly, loving, meek, and pure,
May I to the end endure;
Be to good alone inclined,
Like the Saviour's perfect mind!

2 "None can to the Father come
But by me, the Living Way."
Saviour, guide us to our home,
And the Father's love display!
"I was once, like you, a child,
And a child's subjection knew."
Teach us, Saviour, to be mild,
Kind, obedient, tender, true!

MINISTRY OF JESUS.

3 "Cup, and cross, and thorny crown
Tell what sorrows I have known."
Saviour, send thy spirit down,
Make thy patience all our own!
"Though in death's repose I lay,
I've ascended to the skies."
Saviour, thou hast led the way,
Teach our spirits how to rise.

103. Mrs. Luke. STORY OF OLD. P.M. F. G. Hume.

I think when I read that sweet sto-ry of old, When Je-sus was here a-mong men,
Yet still to his pres-ence in faith I may go, And ask for a share of his love;

How he call'd lit-tle chil-dren, as lambs, to his fold, I should like to have been with him then.
For he who loved children when dwelling below Still loves them when dwelling a-bove.

I wish that his hand had been placed on my head, That his arm had been thrown around me;
But many dear children have nev-er been told That they his dis-ci-ples may be:

And that I might have seen his kind look when he said, "Let the little ones come unto me!"
I should like them to hear that sweet say-ing of old, "Let the little ones come unto me!"

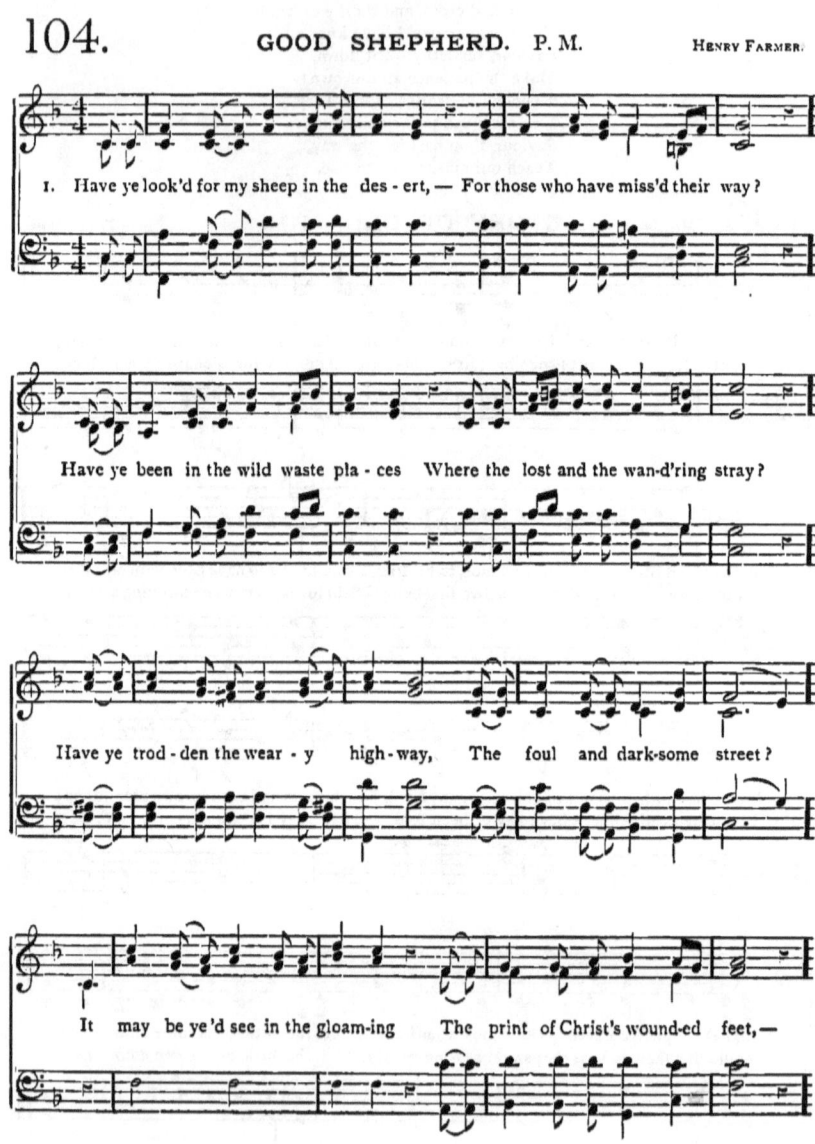

MINISTRY OF JESUS.

It may be ye'd see in the gloam-ing The print of Christ's wound-ed feet.

2 Have ye folded close to your bosom
   The trembling, neglected lamb,
   And taught to the little wand'rer
   The sweet sound of the Shepherd's name?
   Have ye search'd for the poor and needy,
   With no clothing, no home, no bread?
   ‖: The Son of Man was among them,—
   He had nowhere to lay his head. :‖

3 Have ye stood by the sad and the weary,
   To watch o'er the couch of death,
   To comfort the sorrow-stricken,
   And to strengthen the feeble faith?
   And have ye ne'er felt when the glory
   Hath stream'd through the open door,
   ‖: And flitted across the dark shadows,
   That Christ had been there before? :‖

105.　　　ST. MICHAEL. S. M.　　　From Genevan Psalter.

1. Be-hold the Prince of Peace, The chos-en of the Lord,
God's well-be-lov-ed Son, ful-fils The sure pro-phet-ic word!

2 Jesus, thou light of men,
   Thy doctrine life imparts;
   Oh, may we feel its quickening power
   To warm and glad our hearts!

3 Cheer'd by its beams, our souls
   Shall run the heav'nly way;
   The path which Christ has mark'd and trod
   Will lead to endless day.

GOD'S CARE AND LOVE.

107. Rev. H. F. Lyte. ST. GEORGE. 7s. D. Sir George J. Elvey.

1. Pleasant are Thy courts above,
In the land of light and love;
Pleasant are Thy courts below,
In this land of joy and woe.
Oh, my spirit longs and faints
For the converse of Thy saints,
For the brightness of Thy face,
King of glory, God of grace!

2 Happy birds that sing and fly
Round Thine altars, O Most High!
Happier souls, that find a rest
In a heav'nly Father's breast!
Like the wand'ring dove that found
No repose on earth around,
They can to their ark repair,
And enjoy it ever there.

3 Happy souls! their praises flow
Even in the vale of woe;
Waters in the desert rise,
Manna feeds them from the skies;
On they go from strength to strength
Till they reach Thy throne at length,
At Thy feet adoring fall
Who hast led them safe through all.

GOD'S CARE AND LOVE.

108. "THOU KNOWEST." 11.10.11.10.10.10. J. BARNBY.

1. Thou know-est, Lord, the wea-ri-ness and sor-row Of each sad heart that comes to Thee for rest; Cares of to-day, and bur-dens for to-mor-row, Bless-ings im-plored, and sins to be con-fessed; We come be-fore Thee at Thy gra-cious word, And lay them at Thy feet: Thou know-est, Lord.

2. Thou know-est all the past: how long and blind-ly, Lost on the moun-tains, the poor wan-d'rer stray'd; How the good Shep-herd fol-low'd, and how kind-ly He bore it home, up-on His shoul-ders laid; And heal'd the bleed-ing wounds, and sooth'd the pain, And brought back life, and hope, and strength a-gain.

3 Thou knowest all the present: each tempta-
tion,
Each toilsome duty, each foreboding fear;
All that to each is given of tribulation,
Or to beloved ones, than self more dear;
All pensive memories, as we journey on,
And longings for the smiles and voices
gone.

4 Thou knowest all the future: gleams of glad-
ness
By stormy clouds too quickly overcast;
Hours of sweet fellowship and parting sadness,
And Death's dark river to be crossed at last.
Oh! what could hope and confidence afford
To tread that path, but this, Thou knowest,
Lord!

GOD'S CARE AND LOVE.

109. F. R. Havergal. CUSTODIA. 10s. F. R. Havergal.

Not too slow.

1. God will take care of you. All thro' the day He is beside you to keep you from ill; Waking or resting, at work or at play, God still is with you, and watches you still.

2. He will take care of you. All thro' the night He, the Good Shepherd, His flock safely keeps; Darkness to Him is the same as the light, He never slumbers, and He never sleeps. A-MEN.

3 He will take care of you all through the year,
Crowning each day with His kindness and love;
Sending you blessings, and shielding from fear,
Leading you on to the bright home above.

4 He will take care of you. Yes; to the end
Nothing can alter His love for His own:
Children, be glad that you have such a Friend;
He will not leave you one moment alone. AMEN.

GOD'S CARE AND LOVE.

110.   INNOCENCE. 8s & 3s.   Maria S. Ragland.

1. I hear a sweet voice ringing clear, All is well!
   It is my Father's voice I hear, All is well!
   Wher-e'er I walk, that voice is heard:
   It is my God's, my Father's word: Fear not, but trust; I am the Lord: All is well!

2. In happy days I love to sing, All is well!
   'Midst sounding songs I spread the wing, All is well!
   I burst from out my prison bars, Nor fear nor hate my
   transport mars, I soar and sing beyond the stars, All is well!

3 But then when darker days come on,
    All is well!
I sigh that I am far from home,
    All is well!
Then, like a dove far from her nest,
I mourn to be forever blest;
I know there is a land of rest:
    All is well!

4 In morning hours serene and bright,
    All is well!
In evening hours or darkening night,
    All is well!
And when at last my hour shall come,
And I on earth shall cease to roam,
Oh, let me sing as I go home,
    All is well!

GOD'S CARE AND LOVE.

111. CHANNING. 7s.
Composed for this Hymnal by R. H. Clouston, Jr.
Allegretto.

1. Hear ye not a voice from heav-en
To the list'ning spir-it giv-en?
"Chil-dren, come!" it seems to say;
"Give your hearts to me to-day!"

2 Father, teach me, day by day,
Love's sweet bidding to obey!
Sweeter lesson cannot be, —
Loving Him who first loved me.

3 With a child-like heart of love,
At Thy bidding may I move;
Prompt to serve and follow Thee, —
Loving Him who first loved me.

112. H. Baker. LOGOS. 6s. German.

1. Lord, Thy word a - bid - eth,
   And our foot-steps guid - eth;
   Who its truth be - liev - eth,
   Light and joy re - ceiv - eth.

2. When the storms are o'er us,
   And dark clouds be - fore us,
   Then its light di - rect - eth,
   And our way pro - tect - eth.

3 Word of mercy, giving
Help unto the living;
Word of life, supplying
Comfort to the dying!

4 Oh that we, discerning
Its most holy learning,
Lord, may love and fear Thee,
Evermore be near Thee!

GOD'S CARE AND LOVE

113. CHORAL. P.M. — Old German.

1. Whate'er my God ordains is right: His holy will abideth;
I will be still, whate'er He doth, And follow where He guideth.
He is my God: Tho' dark my road, He holds me that I shall not fall, —
Wherefore to Him I leave it all.

2 Whate'er my God ordains is right:
  He never will deceive me;
He leads me by the proper path,
  I know He will not leave me;
    And take, content,
    What He hath sent.
His hand can turn my grief away,
And patiently I wait His day.

3 Whate'er my God ordains is right:
  Here shall my stand be taken;
Though sorrow, need, or death be mine,
  Yet am I not forsaken;
    My Father's care
    Is round me there.
He holds me that I shall not fall,
And so to Him I leave it all.

GOD'S CARE AND LOVE.

114. ADELAIDE A. PROCTOR. **PROCTOR.** 8s & 4s. 6 lines. J. L. NAYLOR.

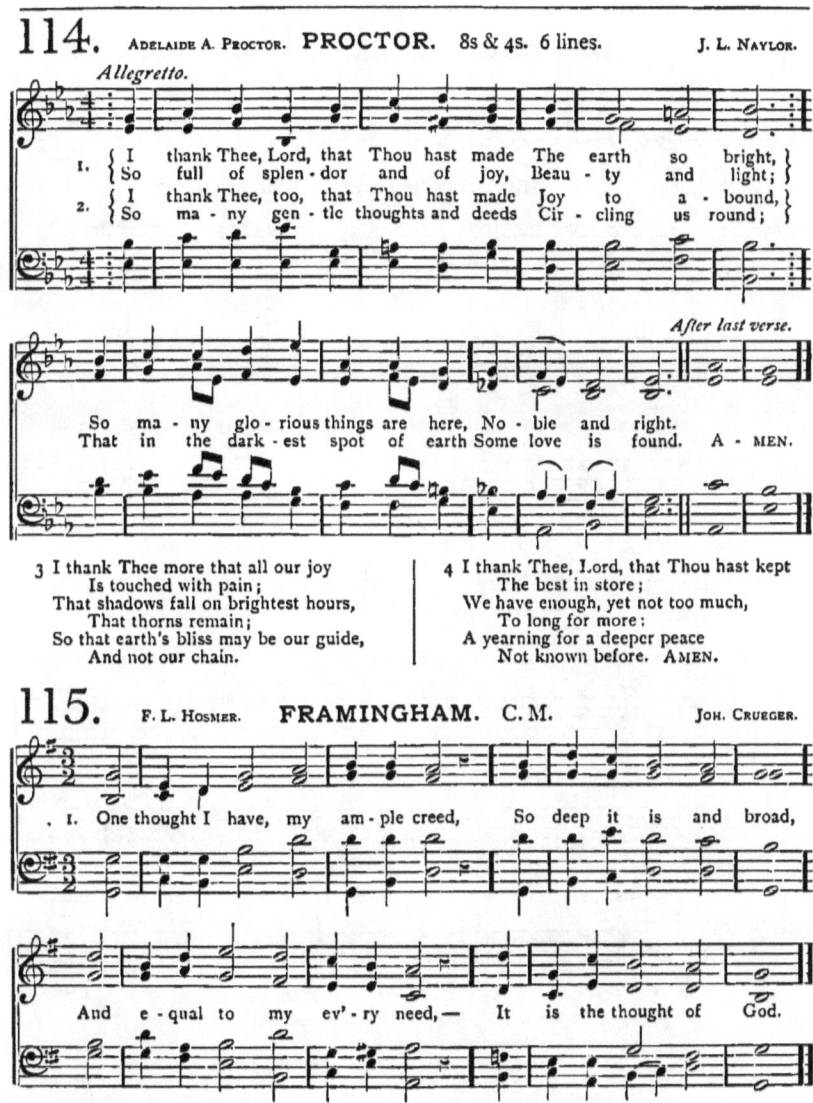

1. { I thank Thee, Lord, that Thou hast made The earth so bright,
     So full of splen-dor and of joy, Beau-ty and light;
2. { I thank Thee, too, that Thou hast made Joy to a-bound,
     So ma-ny gen-tle thoughts and deeds Cir-cling us round;

   So ma-ny glo-rious things are here, No-ble and right.
   That in the dark-est spot of earth Some love is found. A-MEN.

3 I thank Thee more that all our joy
    Is touched with pain;
  That shadows fall on brightest hours,
    That thorns remain;
  So that earth's bliss may be our guide,
    And not our chain.

4 I thank Thee, Lord, that Thou hast kept
    The best in store;
  We have enough, yet not too much,
    To long for more:
  A yearning for a deeper peace
    Not known before. AMEN.

115. F. L. HOSMER. **FRAMINGHAM.** C. M. JOH. CRUEGER.

1. One thought I have, my am-ple creed, So deep it is and broad,
   And e-qual to my ev'-ry need,— It is the thought of God.

2 I ask not far before to see,
    But take in trust my road;
  Life, death, and immortality
    Are in my thought of God.

3 Be still the light upon my way,
    My pilgrim staff and rod,
  My rest by night, my strength by day,
    O blessed thought of God!

GOD'S CARE AND LOVE.

116. W. C. Gannett.   **HOLY PLACE.** C. M. D.   H. G. Spaulding.

1. The Lord is in His Holy Place, In all things, near and far;
Shekinah of the snow-flake, He, And glory of the star.
And secret of the April land, That stirs the field to flowers,
Where little Bethels bud and bloom To hold Him thro' the hours.

2 He hides Himself within the love
Of those that we love best;
The smiles and tones that make our homes
Are shrines by Him possessed.
He tents within the lonely heart,
And shepherds every thought:
We find Him not by seeking long,
We lose Him not unsought.

GOD'S CARE AND LOVE.

117. Mrs. E. H. Leland. **AUXILIUM.** 8.7.8.7.7.5. T. R. Matthews.

1. Oh, the Father's hands are helping In the work you have to do! Have you never felt them lifting When the task was hard for you? There is help for the faithful, There is help for you.

2 Though the day be dark with sorrow,
   And the way be hard and long,
   Yet His love shall light the morrow,
   In His strength you will be strong.
      There is help for the faithful, etc.

3 What your hands find good in doing,
   Do you, then, with all your might;
   Though the work be plain and lowly,
   It is blessèd in His sight.
      There is help for the faithful, etc.

4 Oh, be patient in your striving!
   "Learn to labor and to wait,"
   And the Father's love shall lead you
   When the way is steep and strait.
      There is help for the faithful, etc.

GOD'S CARE AND LOVE.

118. Rev. J. Page Hopps. **VOX PATRIS.** P. M. H. Smart.

1. Hark, hark, my soul! thy Father's voice is calling,—E'en now it breathes o'er life's dark troubled sea; That gracious voice like heav'nly dew is falling: Hark, hark, my soul! the Father calls for thee. Father of mercy, Father of love! Thee would we follow to our own dear home above!

2 Hark, hark, my soul! from heav'n that voice is pleading
   With thee, ere evil days draw darkly near;
   Now, in thy dawn, the Father's hand is leading
   From sin and shame, from sorrow, doubt, and fear.
      Father of mercy, etc.

3 Hark, hark, my soul! still, still, that voice is sounding
   Like music sweet from some far distant shore;
   While angel bands, our daily path surrounding,
   Lead God's dear children on forevermore.
      Father of mercy, etc.

PRAYER AND TRUST.

119. NEWTON. 7s.
Lyra Germanica.
Composed for this Hymnal by R. H. Clouston, Jr.

1. As a bird in mead-ow fair, Or in lone-ly for-est, sings,
Till it fills the sum-mer air, And the green-wood sweet-ly rings,—
So my heart to Thee would raise, O my God, its song of praise,
That the gloom of night is o'er, And I see the sun once more.

2 If Thou, Sun of Love, arise,
  All my heart with joy is stirr'd;
And to greet Thee upward flies,
  Gladsome as yon little bird.
Shine Thou in me clear and bright
Till I learn to praise Thee right;
Guide me in the narrow way,
Let me ne'er in darkness stray.

3 Bless to-day whate'er I do,
  Bless whate'er I have and love;
From the paths of virtue true
  Let me never, never rove.
By Thy Spirit strengthen me
In the faith that leads to Thee;
Then, an heir of life on high,
Fearless I may live and die.

PRAYER AND TRUST.

120. Bp. W. How. GUIDANCE. 7s. 6 lines. G. A. Macfarren.

1. Lord, Thy children guide and keep, As with feeble steps they press On the pathway, rough and steep, Thro' the weary wilderness. Holy Father, day by day Lead, O lead us in the narrow way!

2. There are stony ways to tread,— Give the strength we sorely lack; There are tangled paths to thread,— Shed Thy light upon the track. Holy Father, etc.

3 There are soft and flow'ry glades
   Deck'd with golden-fruited trees,
  Sunny slopes, and scented shades:
   Keep us, Lord, from slothful ease.
     Holy Father, etc.

4 Upward still to purer heights,
   Onward yet to scenes more blest,
  Calmer regions, clearer lights,
   Till we reach the promised rest.
     Holy Father, etc. AMEN.

PRAYER AND TRUST.

121. EXCELSIOR. P. M.

Composed for this Hymnal by E. H. Bailey.

1. High-er, high-er, will we climb Up the mount of glo-ry,
That our names may live through time In our coun-try's sto-ry!
Hap-py, when her wel-fare calls, He who con-quers, he who falls!
High-er, high-er, let us climb Up the mount of glo-ry!

2 Onward, onward may we press
   Through the path of duty!
Virtue is true happiness,
   Excellence true beauty.
Minds are of celestial birth:
Make we, then, a heaven of earth.
Onward, onward may we press
   Through the path of duty!

PRAYER AND TRUST.

122. S. D. Phelps.   PRAYER. P. M.   Wesleyan Tune-Book.

1. Father, Thy boundless love Thou givest me, Nor should I aught withhold, dear Lord, from Thee; In love my soul would bow, My heart fulfil its vow, Some off'ring bring Thee now, Something for Thee!

2 My feeble faith looks up, Father, to Thee!
Grant me in darkness still Thy light to see;
Help me my cross to bear,
Thy wondrous love declare,
Some song to raise, or prayer,
Something for Thee!

3 Give me a faithful heart, — faithful to Thee,
That each departing day henceforth may see
Some work of love begun,
Some deed of kindness done,
Some wand'rer sought and won,
Something for Thee!

123. Anna L. Waring.   ASPIRATION. P. M.   Henry Farmer.

1. I know, O Father, all my life Is portioned out for me, ...
2. I ask Thee for a thoughtful love, Thro' constant watching wise, ...

PRAYER AND TRUST.

And chang-es that are sure to come I do not fear to see;...
To meet the glad with joy-ful smiles, And wipe the weep-ing eyes,—

I ask Thee for a pres-ent mind In-tent on pleas-ing Thee....
A heart at lei-sure from it-self, To soothe and sym-pa-thize....

Oh, fill my heart! Thy grace im-part,— A sure sup-port for me!...
Oh, fill my heart! Thy grace im-part! Bid kind-ly thoughts a-rise!..

Oh, fill my heart! Thy grace im-part,— A sure sup-port for me!
Oh, fill my heart! Thy grace im-part! Bid kind-ly thoughts a-rise!

3 I would not have the restless will
   That hurries to and fro,
That seeks for something great to do,
   Some secret thing to know;
I would be treated as a child,
   And guided where I go.
      Oh, fill my heart!
      This faith impart,
   That I its peace may know!

4 In service which Thy will appoints
   There are no bonds for me;
My inmost heart is taught that truth
   Which makes Thy children free,—
A life of self-renouncing love,
   This life is liberty.
      Oh, fill my heart!
      This love impart,
   My soul's true joy to be!

PRAYER AND TRUST.

124. Isaac Williams.   PEACE. 8.8.8.4.8.4.   T. L. Selby.

1. The child leans on its parent's breast, Leaves there its cares, and is at rest; The bird sits singing by his nest, And tells aloud His trust in God, and so is blest 'Neath ev'ry cloud.

2 He has no store, he sows no seed,
Yet sings aloud and doth not heed;
By flowing stream and grassy mead
  He sings God's praise.
And shall not we in ev'ry need
  Our prayer upraise?

3 The heart that trusts forever sings,
And feels as light as it had wings;
A well of peace within it springs.
  Come good or ill,
Whate'er to-day, to-morrow, brings,
  It is His will.

125. William Everett.   TENDERNESS. S. M.   Charles Steggall.

1. Deal gently with us, Lord! The ways of sin are wide;
2. Deal gently with us, Lord! Our foes press thick and bold;

PRAYER AND TRUST.

After last verse.

Oh, take us by Thy ten-der hand, And in Thy path-way guide!
Oh, who shall fight the war-fare through If Thou Thine arm with-hold? A - MEN.

3 Deal gently with us, Lord!
  For Christ, Thy Son, was kind;
  Oh, watch Thou kindly o'er the sheep
  He left in grief behind!

4 Deal gently with us, Lord!
  Then we shall gentle be;
  And o'er our feeble brethren watch
  In love and charity. AMEN.

126. Rev. H. F. LYTE.   PAX DEI. 10s.   Rev. J. B. DYKES.

1. I need Thy presence, Lord, each pass-ing hour: What but Thy grace can foil the tempt-er's pow'r? Who like Thy-self my guide and stay can be?

After last verse.

Through cloud and sun-shine, oh, a-bide with me! A - MEN.

2 Come not in terrors as the King of kings,
  But kind and good, with healing in Thy wings;
  Pity for tears, a heart for ev'ry plea:
  Come, loving Father, thus abide with me!

3 I fear no foe with Thee at hand to bless;
  Ills have no weight, and tears no bitterness:
  Where is Death's sting? where, Grave, thy victory?
  I triumph still if Thou abide with me! AMEN.

PRAYER AND TRUST.

127.   RHODES. S.M.   C. W. Jordan.

1. One gift, my God, I seek: To know Thee always near;
2. Wher-e'er I go, my God, Oh, let me find Thee there!

To feel Thy hand, to see Thy face, Thy bless-ed voice to hear.
Wher-e'er I stay, stay Thou with me,— A pres-ence ev'-ry-where.

3 And if Thou bringest peace,
  Or if Thou bringest pain,
But come Thyself with all that comes,
  And all shall go for gain.

4 Long list'ning to Thy words,
  My voice shall catch Thy tone,
And, lock'd in Thine, my hand shall grow
  All loving like Thine own.

128. J. Keble.   HURSLEY. L.M.   Arr. by W. H. Monk.

1. Sun of my soul, for ev-er near, It is not night if Thou be here;

Oh, may no earth-born cloud a-rise To hide Thee from Thy ser-vant's eyes!

2 When the soft dews of kindly sleep
  My wearied eyelids gently steep,
  Be my last thought, how sweet to rest
  Upon my loving Father's breast!

3 Abide with me from morn till eve,
  For without Thee I cannot live;
  Abide with me when night is nigh,
  For without Thee I dare not die.

PRAYER AND TRUST.

129. F. L. Hosmer. **PSALM OF TRUST. C. M.** German.

1. I little see, I little know, Yet can I fear no ill:
   He who hath guid-ed me till now Will be my lead-er still.
2. No bur-den yet was on me laid Of trou-ble or of care,
   But He my trem-bling step hath stay'd, And given me strength to bear.

3 Upon His providence I lean,
  As lean in faith I must:
  The lesson of my life hath been
  A heart of grateful trust.

4 And so my onward way I fare
  With happy heart and calm,
  And mingle with my daily care
  The music of my psalm.

130. **ST. AGNES. C. M.** Rev. J. B. Dykes.

1. Thou, Lord of life, whose ten-der care Hath led us on till now,
   We in this qui-et hour of pray'r Be-fore Thy pres-ence bow!

2 Thou, blessed God, hast been our Guide,
  Through life our Guard and Friend!
  Oh still, on life's uncertain tide,
  Preserve us to the end!

3 To Thee our grateful praise we bring
  For mercies day by day;
  Lord, teach our hearts Thy love to sing;
  Lord, teach us how to pray!

PRAYER AND TRUST.

131. MORE LOVE TO THEE. P.M.

Composed for this Hymnal by E. H. Bailey.

1. More love, O God, to Thee, More love to Thee!

Hear Thou the prayer I raise On bend-ed knee!

This is my ear-nest plea,— More love, O God, to Thee,

More love, O God, to Thee, More love to Thee!

2 Once earthly joy I craved,
    Sought peace and rest;
 Now Thee alone I seek:
    Give what is best.
 This all my prayer shall be,—
 ||: More love, O God, to Thee, :||
    More love to Thee !

3 Then shall my latest breath
    Whisper Thy praise;
 This be the parting cry
    My heart shall raise,
 This its petition be, —
 ||: More love, O God, to Thee, :||
    More love to Thee !

3 There let the way appear
  Steps unto heaven;
  All that Thou sendest me
  In mercy given;
  Angels to beckon me
  Nearer, my God, to Thee,
  ||: Nearer to Thee! :||

4 Or if, on joyful wing
  Cleaving the sky,
  Sun, moon, and stars forgot,
  Upward I fly,
  Still all my song shall be,—
  Nearer, my God, to Thee,
  ||: Nearer to Thee! :||

PRAYER AND TRUST.

133. MISERICORDIA. 7s & 6s. D.

Rev. W. H. Furness, D.D.
Sir Arthur S. Sullivan.

1. Have mercy, O our Father! For unto Thee we cry;
Faint, weary, weak, and way-worn, Unto Thy wings we fly.
Speak peace to us, Thy children, For without Thee we die;
Speak peace to us, Thy children, For without Thee we die.

2 We go forth in the darkness,
 Oh, grant to us Thy light!
We wander from the pathway
 Bewilder'd in the night.
‖: Oh, be Thou still our Shepherd,
 And lead us on aright! :‖

PRAYER AND TRUST.

134. LEAD ME, MY FATHER. 11s.

Rev. J. Page Hopps.
Composed for this Hymnal by E. H. Bailey.

1. Oh, lead me, my Father, lead Thou, lest I stray!
Oh, lead Thou me onward where Thou wilt each day!
All passion be silent, all self-will be still,
And meekly my spirit ask only Thy will!

2 'Mid life's sweetest pleasures, Lord, keep me Thine own,
Lest I should forget Thee, or duty disown;
When sorrow o'erwhelms me, and gone is the light,
Then shine on me, Father, make Thou my way bright.

3 When thought is a burden, when work is a care,
Oh, then let me cherish the sweetness of prayer!
When shadows are falling, when earth's day is past,
Oh, lead me, my Father, to sunshine at last!

PRAYER AND TRUST.

135. NEAR TO THEE. 7s. 6 lines.

Rev. T. A. Stowell.   A. Zoellner.

1. Father, we are young and weak, Yet we have a race to run; Glorious is the crown we seek, Hard the fight that must be won! Lest we faint, and lest we flee, Keep us ever near to Thee! Keep us ever near to Thee!

2 Many are our foes and strong, —
Foes without, and fears within;
Great temptations to go wrong,
And become the slaves of sin.
We shall surely conquered be
|: If we keep not near to Thee. :||

3 When the prize of victory's won,
And the hard-fought contest o'er,
We shall hear the glad "Well done!"
On the shining heavenly shore,
And through all eternity
||: Evermore be near to Thee! :||

WARFARE OF LIFE.

136. VOX DEI. 7s & 6s. 12 lines. S. W. WILKINSON.

1. There lives a voice within me, Guest-angel of my heart,
Whose whisp'rings strive to win me To act a manful part.
Up evermore it springeth, Like some sweet melody;
And evermore it singeth This sacred truth to me:
This world is full of beauty, The coldest heart to move;
And if we did our duty, It might be full of love.

2 The leaf-tongues of the forest,
   The flower-lips of the sod,
   The birds that hymn their raptures
   Up to the throne of God,
   The summer wind that bringeth
   The music of the sea, —
   Have each a voice that singeth
   This blessed truth to me:
       This world is full of beauty, etc.

3 Oh, voice of God most tender!
   Oh, voice of God divine!
   Still be my heart's defender,
   Till every thought is Thine.
   My soul in gladness bringeth
   Its song of praise to Thee;
   While all around me singeth
   This holy truth to me:
       This world is full of beauty, etc.

137. LIFE'S VOYAGE. P.M.

1. O'er the wide and rest-less ocean Of our life we speed a-long,
And to God, whose mer-cy wafts us, Will we raise our trust-ful song.

CHORUS.
Sail-ing, sail-ing o-ver the sea, In storm and sun-shine bright,
Bound for Par-a-dise are we, The land of true de-light!

2 Never fear the angry surges
   Beating o'er the reefs of sin;
But obey the voice of duty,
   Keep alert the watch within.
      Sailing, sailing, etc.

3 For our home is o'er the waters,
   On a fair but distant strand;
And the Saviour is the pilot
   Who will bring us safe to land.
      Sailing, sailing, etc.

WARFARE OF LIFE.

138. COME, LABOR ON! P. M.

Words adapted by H. G. S.   Arranged for this Hymnal by J. B. Gilman.

1. Come, labor on! Come, labor on! Who dares stand idle on the plain While all around us waves the grain, The golden grain for harvest? Work with the reapers, Go, work to-day; No arm but may do service here! Away with gloomy doubt and fear!

2 Come, labor on! Come, labor on!
By human love will God fulfil
His righteous and His blessed will,
And gather in His harvest.
  Work with the reapers,
  Go, work to-day;
The workmen few, the field so wide,
New laborers still must be supplied.
  Come, labor on! etc.

3 Come, labor on! Come, labor on!
No rest till evening's shadows lie
Along our pathway to the sky,
And ended is earth's harvest.
  Work with the reapers,
  Go, work to-day,—
Till, with the setting of the sun,
We hear the welcome words, "Well done!"
  Come, labor on! etc.

WARFARE OF LIFE.

139. LITTLE BY LITTLE. P.M.

LEON HERBERT.   Composed for this Hymnal by E. H. BAILEY.

1. Lit-tle by lit-tle the time goes by; Lit-tle by lit-tle the mo-ments fly;
2. Lit-tle by lit-tle the skies grow clear; Lit-tle by lit-tle the sun comes near;

Lit-tle by lit-tle, an hour, a day, Num-bers its min-utes, and flees a-way;
Lit-tle by lit-tle the days smile out Glad-der and bright-er on pain and doubt;

Lit-tle by lit-tle the race is run,— Trouble, and waiting, and toil are done.
Lit-tle by lit-tle the seed we sow In-to a beau-ti-ful flow'r will grow.

3 Little by little the world grows strong,
Fighting the battle of Right and Wrong;
Little by little the Wrong gives way,—
Little by little the Right has sway;
Little by little all longing souls
Struggle up nearer the shining goals.

4 Little by little the good in men
Blossoms to beauty for human ken;
Little by little the angels see
Prophecies better of good to be;
Little by little the God of all
Lifts the world nearer His pleading call.

140. STRIVE, WAIT, AND PRAY. P.M.

ADELAIDE A. PROCTOR.   HENRY FARMER.

1. Strive! yet I do not prom-ise The prize you dream of to-day

WARFARE OF LIFE.

2 Wait! yet I do not tell you
  The Hour you long for now
  Will not come with its radiance vanish'd,
  And a shadow upon its brow;
  Yet far through the misty future,
  With a crown of starry light,
  ‖: An Hour of joy you know not
  Is winging her silent flight. :‖

3 Pray! though the gift you ask for
  May never comfort your fears,
  May never repay your pleading,
  Yet pray, and with hopeful tears;
  An answer, not that you long for,
  But diviner, will come one day.
  ‖: Your eyes are too dim to see it;
  Yet strive, and wait, and pray. :‖

WARFARE OF LIFE.

141. LIFE'S MEANING. 8s & 7s.
Composed for this Hymnal by R. H. Clouston, Jr.

Spirited.

1. Life is not a fleet-ing shad-ow, Or a wave up-on the beach;
2. Life is ours for faith-ful la-bor Of the hand or of the thought;

Tho' our days be swift, yet last-ing Is the stamp we give to each.
Ev' - ry hour and ev' - ry mo-ment Is with liv-ing mean-ing fraught.

3 Waking every morn to duty,
Ere its hours shall pass away,
Let some act of love and service
Mark it as a holy day.

4 Work! our Father worketh ever.
He who works not cannot play;
Work for use and work for beauty;
So sweet rest shall crown each day.

142. TILDEN. 6.6.4.6.6.6.4.
Rev. W. P. Tilden.
Composed for this Hymnal by E. H. Bailey.

1. Strong in the liv-ing God, Strong for His work and word,

Be ev' - ry heart; Strong for the true and right, Strong for the

WARFARE OF LIFE.

Chris-tian fight, Strong with ce-les-tial might To do our part.

2 May the quick word of God,
By which the true have trod
In virtue strong,
Abide in us with pow'r,
Guiding in ev'ry hour,
Making each soul a tow'r
'Gainst Sin and Wrong.

3 So may we overcome
All wrong in heart, in home,
In country dear;
Loyal to truth and love,
May we our manhood prove,
Trusting in God above
With heart sincere.

143. NEW SOUTH. L. M.

Rev. W. P. TILDEN.   Composed for this Hymnal by E. H. BAILEY.

1. Gird Thou our souls, O God of might! To bat-tle for the true and right,
2. Thy liv-ing word be our com-mand For for-ward march or fear-less stand,

And give us that Dam-as-can blade Of faith and mor-al cour-age made.
For bold re-sist-ance to the wrong, In sin-gle hand or pha-lanx strong!

3 This world is Thine to utmost bound,
'T is not for Satan's camping-ground;
We face the foe, we draw the sword,
We join the army of the Lord,

4 We lift our banners in Thy name!
With holy zeal our hearts inflame
To stand with Thee, in purpose strong,
Till earth shall hear the angels' song.

144. CHRISTIAN UNION. 7s & 6s. D.

H. G. Spaulding. Samuel Smith.

1. In hearts from sin de-liv-ered God's king-dom com-eth still,
And "peace on earth" a-bid-eth With men of kind-ly will.
Yet must we, still pur-su-ing The way the Mas-ter trod,
Be work-ers in up-build-ing The king-dom of our God.

2 Not ours to see the morning
  Of Love's unclouded day;
Not ours the glorious vision
  Of that for which we pray.
For other generations
  We sow to-day the seed,
And ages that are coming
  Shall reap each golden deed.

3 Then raise the swelling anthem
  Of human brotherhood,
And tell to all the nations
  The joy of doing good.
On earth, as in the heavens,
  The will divine is done;
On earth the kingdom cometh
  Of God's beloved Son.

WARFARE OF LIFE.

145. S. Dyer.   **LABOR.** 7.6.7.5. D.   Rev. C. J. Dickinson.

1. Work, for the night is coming; Work thro' the morn-ing hours;
Work while the dew is spark-ling; Work 'mid spring-ing flow'rs;
Work when the day grows bright-er; Work in the glow-ing sun;
Work, for the night is com-ing, When man's work is done. A-MEN.

After last verse.

2 Work, for the night is coming;
　Work through the sunny noon;
　Fill brightest hours with labor,
　Rest comes sure and soon.
　Give every flying minute
　Something to keep in store;
　Work, for the night is coming,
　When man works no more.

3 Work, for the night is coming
　Under the sunset skies;
　While their bright tints are glowing,
　Work, for daylight flies;
　Work till the last beam fadeth,
　Fadeth to shine no more;
　Work, while the night is darkening,
　When man's work is o'er. AMEN.

WARFARE OF LIFE.

146. PSALM OF LIFE. 6s & 5s. D.
W. H. Monk.

1. Life is onward,— use it
With a forward aim;
Toil is heav'n-ly,— choose it,
And its warfare claim.
Life is onward,— try it,
Ere the day is lost;
It has virtue,— buy it,
At whatever cost.

2 Life is onward, — heed it
In each varied dress;
Your own heart can speed it
On to happiness.
His bright pinion o'er you,
Time waves not in vain,
If Hope chants before you
Her prophetic strain.

WARFARE OF LIFE.

147. DOMINI MILITES. 6s & 5s. D.

Frances R. Havergal. E. J. Hopkins.

1. Who is on the Lord's side? Who will serve the King? Who will be His helpers Other lives to bring? Who will leave the world's side? Who will face the foe? Who is on the Lord's side? Who for Him will go? We are on the Lord's side, We will serve the King; We will be His helpers Other lives to bring!

2 Fierce may be the conflict,
　Strong may be the foe,
But the King's own army
　None can overthrow.
Round His standard ranging,
　Victory is secure,
For His truth unchanging
　Makes the triumph sure.
　　We are on the Lord's side, etc.

3 Not for weight of glory,
　Not for crown and palm,
Enter we the army,
　Raise the warrior psalm;—
In this service royal,
　Love shall ne'er grow cold;
Let us be right loyal,
　Noble, true, and bold.
　　We are on the Lord's side, etc.

148. LIFE'S CONFLICT. 8s & 7s.

Rev. Samuel Johnson. — Tyrolean.

1. On-ward, on-ward, though the re-gion Where thou art be drear and lone;
God hath set a guard-ian le-gion Ver-y near thee: press thou on!
Up-ward, up-ward! Their ho-san-na Roll-eth o'er thee, "God is Love!"
All a-round thy red-cross ban-ner Streams the ra-diance from a-bove.

2 By the thorn-road, and no other,
　Is the Mount of Vision won;
Tread it without shrinking, brother!
　Jesus trod it: press thou on!
By thy trustful calm endeavor,
　Guiding, cheering, like the sun,
Earth-bound hearts thou shalt deliver;
　Oh, for their sake, press thou on!

3 Be this world the wiser, stronger,
　For thy life of pain and peace;
While it needs thee, oh, no longer
　Pray thou for thy quick release;
Pray thou, undisheartened, rather,
　That thou be a faithful son;
By the prayer of Jesus, — "Father,
　Not my will, but Thine, be done!"

WARFARE OF LIFE.

149.   ONE BY ONE.   8s & 7s. D.

Adelaide A. Proctor.   Composed for this Hymnal by E. H. Bailey.

1. One by one the sands are flow-ing, One by one the mo-ments fall;
Some are com-ing, some are go-ing: Do not strive to grasp them all.
One by one thy du-ties wait thee; Let thy whole strength go to each:
Let no fu-ture dreams e-late thee; Learn thou first what these can teach.

2 One by one — bright gifts from Heaven —
   Joys are sent thee here below;
   Take them readily when given,
   Ready too to let them go.
     One by one thy duties, etc.

3 Ev'ry hour that fleets so slowly
   Has its task to do or bear;
   Luminous the crown, and holy,
   When each gem is set with care.
     One by one thy duties, etc.

GOOD WORKS.

150. ST. HUGH. C.M. E. J. Hopkins.

1. Speak gently! it is bet-ter far To rule by love than fear;
Speak gently! let no harsh word mar The good we may do here.

2 Speak gently to the erring ones!
We yet may lead them back,
With holy words and loving tones,
From misery's thorny track.

3 Speak gently! 't is a little thing
Dropp'd in the heart's deep well;
The good, the joy, that it may bring,
Eternity shall tell.

151. WORK FOR ALL. P. M. John Adcock.

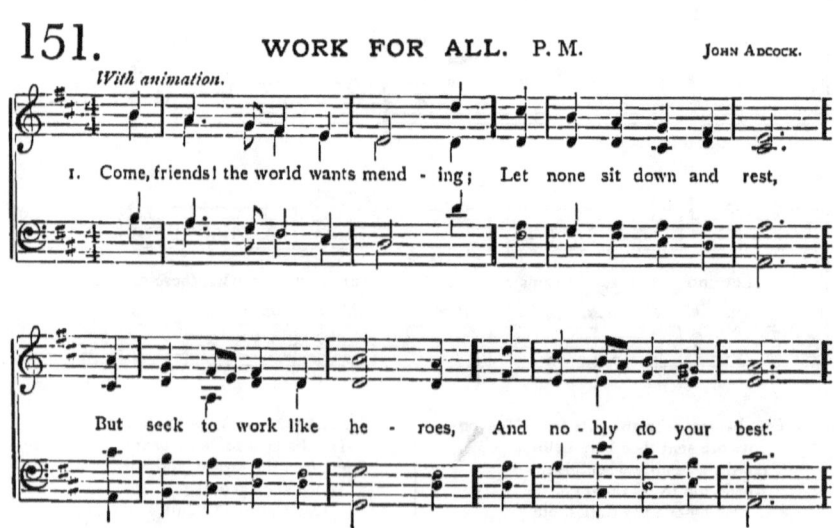

With animation.

1. Come, friends! the world wants mend-ing; Let none sit down and rest,
But seek to work like he-roes, And no-bly do your best.

GOOD WORKS.

Do what you can for fel-low-man, With hon-est heart and true;
Much may be done by ev'-ry one, There's work for all to do.
Come, friends! the world wants mend-ing; Let none sit down and rest,
But seek to work like he-roes, And no-bly do your best.

2 Though you can do but little,
   That little 's something still;
   You 'll find a way for something,
   If you but have the will.
   Now bravely fight for what is right,
   And God will help you through;
   Much may be done by ev'ry one,
     There 's work for all to do.
      Come, friends! etc.

3 Be kind to those around you,
   To charity hold fast;
   Let each think first of others,
   And leave himself till last.
   Act as you would that others should
   Act always unto you;
   Much may be done by ev'ry one,
     There 's work for all to do.
      Come, friends! etc.

GOOD WORKS.

152. FATHERLAND. S.M.
J. S. Bach.

1. Come, brothers, let us go!
   Our Father is our guide;
   And if our way be bright or dark,
   He's ever at our side.

2 The strong be quick to raise
  The weaker when they fall;
  Let love and peace and patience bloom
  In ready help for all.

3 Come, brothers, let us go!
  We travel hand in hand;
  Each with his brother walks in joy
  Through this dear Fatherland.

153. GOLDEN RULE. P.M.
Frank L. Moir.

1. Never lose the golden rule,
   Keep it still in view:
   Do to others as you would
   They should do to you.

GOOD WORKS.

2 Help the feeble ones along,
   Cheer the faint and weak;
   To the sorrow-laden heart
   Words of comfort speak.
   From the bounty of your store
   Freely, freely give;
   Help the struggling and the poor
   Better lives to live.
      Never lose the golden rule, etc.

3 Love the Lord — the first command —
   With thy soul and mind;
   Love thy neighbor as thyself, —
   Both in one combined.
   With each other strive to live
   Justly evermore;
   Always willing to forgive
   Those who grace implore.
      Never lose the golden rule, etc.

3 Down in the human heart, crushed by the tempter,
   Feelings lie buried that grace can restore;
   Touched by a loving heart, wakened by kindness,
   Chords that were broken will vibrate once more.
   Rescue the perishing, etc.

GOOD WORKS.

155. TRUTH. 7s & 5s. HAYDN.

1. Speak the truth! for that is right, What-so-e'er be-fall;
Let your hearts be clear as light, O-pen un-to all!
Oh, be hon-est in your youth! Those who have de-ceived,
E-ven when they speak the truth, Will not be be-lieved.

2 Speak the truth! for God is true,
And your voice is heard;
He is watching over you,
Marking every word.
Pray to Him, for by His might,
And by that alone,
Every sin with which you fight
Can be overthrown.

GOOD WORKS.

156. HELPFULNESS. P. M.

Composed for this Hymnal by E. H. BAILEY.

1. There are lonely hearts to cherish While the days are going by;
There are weary souls that perish While the days are going by.
If a smile we can renew, As our journey we pursue,
Oh, the good we all may do While the days are going by!

2 There's no time for idle scorning
  While the days are going by;
Be our faces like the morning,
  While the days are going by.
Oh, the world is full of sighs,
Full of sad and weeping eyes!
Help the fallen one to rise
  While the days are going by!

3 All the loving links that bind us,—
  While the days are going by,—
One by one we leave behind us,
  While the days are going by!
But the seeds of good we sow,
Both in sun and shade will grow,
And will keep our hearts aglow
  While the days are going by!

GOOD WORKS.

157. LET IT PASS! P. M. — C. H. Purday.

1. Be not swift to take offence,— Let it pass! Anger is a foe to sense,— Let it pass! let it pass! Brood not darkly o'er a wrong, Which will disappear ere long; Rather sing this cheery song,— Let it pass! let it pass!

2 Echo not an angry word,—
   Let it pass!
Think how often you have erred,—
   Let it pass!
Since our joys must pass away
Like the dewdrops on the spray,
Wherefore should our sorrow stay?
   Let it pass!

3 If for good you suffer ill,—
   Let it pass!
Oh, be kind and gentle still.—
   Let it pass!
Time at last makes all things straight;
Let us not resent, but wait,
And our triumph will be great:
   Let it pass!

GOOD WORKS.

158. Rev. C. T. Brooks.   **CHARITY.** 7s.

1. Raise a glad and grateful song,
   Children of the loving God!
   Still, with patient hearts and strong,
   Scatt'ring seed of love abroad.

2. Wet with Pity's human tear,
   Warm'd with Mercy's heav'nly ray,
   It shall spring, sad hearts to cheer,—
   Bloom, to light the lonely way.

3 On Love's errands as ye go
  Through dark paths of Misery's land,
  Helping want and soothing woe
  With soft word and kindly hand,—

4 Unseen blessings throng your way;
  Angels, hid in Woe's dark guise,
  Shall, in heav'nly light, one day
  Stand reveal'd before your eyes.

159. John Taylor.   **GOOD WORKS.** 7s.   W. H. Monk.

1. Lord, what off'rings shall we bring
   At Thine altars when we bow?
   Hearts, the pure, unsullied spring
   Whence the kind affections flow;

2 Willing hands to lead the blind,
  Bind the wounded, feed the poor;
  Love, embracing all our kind,
  Charity, with liberal store.

3 Teach us, O Thou heav'nly King!
  Thus to show our grateful mind,
  Thus the accepted offering bring,—
  Love to Thee and all mankind.

GOOD WORKS.

160. GIVING. 6s & 5s. D.

ADELAIDE A. PROCTOR.   SAMUEL SMITH.

1. See the rivers flowing Downward to the sea,
Pouring all their treasures Bountiful and free:
Yet, to help their giving, Hidden springs arise;
Or, if need be, showers Feed them from the skies!

2 Watch the princely flowers
  Their rich fragrance spread,
Load the air with perfumes,
  From their beauty shed:
Yet their lavish spending
  Leaves them not in dearth,
With fresh life replenished
  By their mother Earth!

3 Give thy heart's best treasures,—
  From fair Nature learn:
Give thy love; and ask not,
  Wait not a return!
And the more thou spendest
  From thy little store,
With a double bounty,
  God will give thee more.

HEAVEN AND HEAVENLY COMFORT.

161. THE TWO WORLDS. 8s & 7s.

A. LAIGHTON. Composed for this Hymnal by E. H. BAILEY.

Slow, with expression.

1. The world is bright and fair, we know, The skies are arch'd in glo-ry;
The stars shine on, the sweet flow'rs blow, And tell their bless-ed sto-ry.

2. But soft-er than the Sum-mer's breath, And fair-er than its ro-ses,
Will be the clime a-far when Death The pear-ly gates un-clo-ses,—

HEAVEN AND HEAVENLY COMFORT.

3. The land where brok-en ties shall twine, And fond hearts will not sev-er,
Where Love's pure light shall bright-er shine For-ev-er and for-ev-er.

162. J. W. Chadwick. **GONE BEFORE.** C. M.   L. Spohr.

1. It sing-eth low in ev'ry heart, We hear it, each and all,—
A song of those who an-swer not, How-ev-er we may call.
2. They throng the si-lence of the breast, We see them as of yore,—
The kind, the brave, the true, the sweet, Who walk with us no more.

3 More home-like seems the vast unknown
  Since they have entered there;
To follow them were not so hard,
  Wherever they may fare.

4 They cannot be where God is not,
  On any sea or shore;
Whate'er betides, Thy love abides,
  Our God, for evermore!

HEAVEN AND HEAVENLY COMFORT.

163. BETTER LAND. 7.5.7.5.7.7.
C. F. ALEXANDER.

1. Ev'ry morn the red sun Rises warm and bright;
But the evening cometh on, And the dark cold night:
There's a bright land far away, Where is never-ending day.

2. Ev'ry spring the sweet young flow'rs Open fresh and gay;
Till the chilly autumn hours Wither them away:
There's a land we have not seen Where the trees are always green. A-MEN.

3 Little birds sing songs of praise
    All the summer long;
But in colder, shorter days,
    They forget their song:
There's a place where angels sing
Ceaseless praises to their King.

4 Who shall go to that bright land?
    All who do the right.
Holy children there shall stand
    In their robes of white.
In that Heaven so bright and blest
Is our everlasting rest. AMEN.

164. F. L. HOSMER. COMFORT. 11.10.11.10. D. S. WEBBE.

1. Father, to Thee we look in all our sorrow: Thou art the

HEAVEN AND HEAVENLY COMFORT.

2 Naught shall affright us, on Thy goodness leaning;
　Low in the heart, Faith singeth still her song;
Chastened by pain, we learn life's deeper meaning;
　And, in our weakness, Thou dost make us strong.
Patient, O heart, though heavy be thy sorrows!
　Be not cast down, disquieted in vain;
Yet shalt thou praise Him, when these darkened furrows,
　Where now He plougheth, wave with golden grain.

HEAVEN AND HEAVENLY COMFORT.

165. F. W. Faber. **O PARADISE!** P.M. J. Barnby.

1. O Paradise! O Paradise! Who doth not crave for rest?
Who would not seek the happy land Where they that loved are blest?

CHORUS.
Where loyal hearts and true Stand ever in the light,
All rapture through and through, In God's most holy sight. A-MEN.

2 O Paradise! O Paradise!
  We want to sin no more;
  We want to be as pure on earth
  As on Thy spotless shore.
    Where loyal hearts, etc.

3 Dear Father, Lord of Paradise!
  Oh, keep us in Thy love,
  And guide us to that happy land
  Of perfect rest above!
    Where loyal hearts, etc.

HEAVEN AND HEAVENLY COMFORT.

166.   NEARER HOME. P. M.
Composed for this Hymnal by A. WHITNEY.

1. One sweet-ly sol-emn thought Comes to me o'er and o'er,— Near-er my part-ing hour am I Than e'er I was be-fore. Near-er home, near-er home! I'm near-er my home to-day Than I've ev-er been be-fore!

2 Father, be Thou my stay,—
Lead me safe and slow!
For it may be that I am nearer home,
Am nearer now than I know.
Nearer home, nearer home!
It may be I 'm nearer my home,—
Yes, nearer now than I know!

HEAVEN AND HEAVENLY COMFORT.

167. Rev. C. T. Brooks. **IN MEMORIAM.** P. M. Mendelssohn.

1. O Father! by Thy holy will Another dear one we resign;
2. God's everlasting arms enfold His children all,—below, above;

Thy will be done! Thy will be done! Help Thou our struggling hearts be still!
Thy will be done! Thy will be done! This shall our trusting hearts uphold:

Was not our loved one also Thine? Thy will be done! Thy will be done!
That we are God's, and God is love! Thy will be done! Thy will be done!

168. **FOR EVER WITH THE LORD.** S. M. D.

J. Montgomery. J. Woodbury.

Not fast.

1. "For ever with the Lord!" Amen, so let it be!

HEAVEN AND HEAVENLY COMFORT.

2 My Father's house on high,
  Home of my soul, how near
At times to Faith's foreseeing eye
  Thy golden gates appear!
    Here in the body pent,
    Absent from Him I roam;
  Yet nightly pitch my moving tent
    A day's march nearer home.
      Nearer home, etc.

3 And then I feel that He,
  Remember'd or forgot,
The Lord, is never far from me,
  Though I perceive Him not.
    Here in the body pent,
    Absent from Him I roam;
  Yet nightly pitch my moving tent
    A day's march nearer home.
      Nearer home, etc.

HEAVEN AND HEAVENLY COMFORT.

169. Rev. H. F. Lyte.   ABIDE WITH ME.   10s.   W. H. Monk.

1. Abide with me! fast falls the even-tide; The darkness deepens; Lord, with me abide! When other helpers fail, and comforts flee, Help of the helpless, oh, abide with me!

2 Swift to its close ebbs out life's little day,
Earth's joys grow dim, its glories pass away;
Change and decay in all around I see:
O Thou who changest not, abide with me!

3 Come, then, in light before my closing eyes!
Shine through the gloom and point me to the skies! [shadows flee
Heaven's morning breaks, and earth's vain
In life and death, O Lord, abide with me!

170.   MELODY. C.M.   German.

1. O God! our help in ages past, Our hope for years to come,
2. Before the hills in order stood, Or earth received her frame,
Our shelter from the storm-y blast, And our e-ter-nal home.
From ev-er-last-ing Thou art God, To end-less years the same. A-MEN.

3 A thousand ages in Thy sight
Are like an evening gone,—
Short as the watch that ends the night
Before the rising sun.

4 O God! our help in ages past,
Our hope for years to come,
Be Thou our God while troubles last,
And our eternal home. AMEN.

HEAVEN AND HEAVENLY COMFORT.

171.   HEAVENLY HOME. 6.4.6.4.6.6.6.4.

Sir Arthur S. Sullivan.

1. We are but pil-grims here, Heav'n is our home;
Trav'l-ing through des-erts drear, Heav'n is our home.
Dan-ger and sor-row stand Round us on ev'-ry hand,
Heav'n is our fa-ther-land, Heav'n is our home. A-MEN.

After last verse.

2 What though the tempests rage?
   Heaven is our home;
Short is our pilgrimage,
   Heaven is our home.
Time's wild and wintry blast
Soon will be overpast,
We shall reach home at last;
   Heaven is our home.

3 Lord, may we murmur not,—
   Heaven is our home,—
Whate'er our earthly lot,
   Heaven is our home.
Grant us at last to stand
There at Thine own Right Hand,
In Thy blest fatherland!
   Heaven is our home. AMEN.

INFANT CLASS SONGS.

172. WHAT IS BIRDIE DOING? 6s & 5s.

EMMA PITT. Composed for this Hymnal by R. H. CLOUSTON, Jr.

1. What is bird-ie do-ing As he hops a-round,
2. What is bird-ie do-ing As he flies a-bove?

Chirp-ing while he's eat-ing Crumbs from off the ground?
Oh, he's sing-ing sweet-ly His bright song of love!

CHORUS. *ff*

Bird-ie's sing-ing prais-es; So will I,— yes, I!
Bird-ie's sing-ing prais-es To his God on high!

3 Birdie says, "God loves me;
  Made my wings to fly;
  Gave me strength to help me
  Soar so near the sky."
  Birdie's singing, etc.

4 Yes, God loves the birdies,
  Loves the children too;
  Gives us food and raiment,
  Parents kind and true.
  Birdie's singing, etc.

INFANT CLASS SONGS.

173. FERRIER. 7s. Rev. J. B. Dykes.

1. What can lit-tle ones like me Find, O Lord, to of-fer Thee?
   On-ly of Thy boun-ty fed, Sup-pliant for my dai-ly bread.
2. Child-like heart of truth shall be Dear-er gift than gold to Thee;
   And its pray'r and psalm shall rise Like sweet in-cense to the skies. A-MEN.

After last verse.

3 Teach me, then, the steps to trace
Of the Saviour full of grace;
All his footsteps as a child,
Holy, harmless, undefiled.

4 Thus, O Lord, in Thy dear love
Fit me for Thy rest above;
Help me, this and ev'ry day,
All Thy precepts to obey! AMEN.

174. HARVEST. P. M. John Adcock.

1. The fields are all white, And the reap-ers are few; We chil-dren are will-ing,
   But what can we do To work for our Lord in His har - vest?
2. Our hands are so small, And our words are so weak, We can-not teach oth-ers;
   How then shall we seek To work for our Lord in His har - vest?

3 We'll work by our prayers,
By the pennies we bring,
By small self-denials,—
The least little thing
May work for our Lord in His harvest.

4 Until, by-and-by,
As the years pass at length,
We too may be reapers,
And go forth in strength
To work for our Lord in His harvest.

INFANT CLASS SONGS.

175.   **CHILDREN'S MITE.** 8s & 7s.

AUGUSTA LARNED.   S. B. SAXTON.

1. Little hands, be free in giving;
   Little hearts, be glad to serve:
   Each unselfish act of living
   God fails never to observe.
   Give not only gold and treasure,
   Give your sympathy and care;
   Love that knew not stint or measure
   Jesus scatter'd ev'rywhere.

2 All the goods your hands can carry
  When you stand with God on high
  Are your blessings to the weary,
  To the sick and poor who sigh.
  Thus you garner up in heaven —
  Children know and ever heed —
  All the joy your lives have given
  To God's little ones in need.

3 Let the sweet and joyful story
  Of the Saviour's wondrous love
  Wake on earth a song of glory,
  Like the Angels' song above.

4 Father, send the glorious hour,
  Every heart be Thine alone!
  For the kingdom and the power
  And the glory are Thine own. AMEN.

INFANT CLASS SONGS.

177. TO AND FRO. P. M.
Henry Tucker.

1. To and fro! to and fro! Hear the tread of little children,
As they go, as they go, — Busy march of busy feet!
Here and there, ev'rywhere, Joyous songs we're singing;
Loud and clear, full of cheer, Happy tones are ringing.

2 To and fro! to and fro!
Hear the tread of little children,
As they go, as they go, —
Busy march of busy feet!
Blithe and gay, all the day,
Early morn till even;
Let us raise songs of praise
To our God in heaven.
    To and fro, to and fro! etc.

ANNIVERSARY.

178. SEASONS. 7s & 6s. D. MENDELSSOHN.

1. The ever-changing seasons In silence come and go;
But Thou, eternal Father, No time or change canst know.
Oh, pour Thy grace upon us, That we may worthier be,
Each year that passes o'er us, To dwell in heav'n with Thee!

2 Oh, by each mercy sent us,
And by each grief and pain,
By blessings like the sunshine,
And sorrows like the rain,
Our barren hearts make fruitful
With every goodly grace,
That we Thy name may hallow,
And see at last Thy face.

ANNIVERSARY.

179. COMMEMORATION. 7s & 6s. D.

Rev. T. A. Stowell.   Matthew Cooke.

1. Come, Christian youths and maidens, Come, brothers, old and young,
Uplift your hearts and voices, Be praise on ev'ry tongue.
Within this house we gather, Our yearly feast to hold;
Come, join our joyful anthem, Ye brothers, young and old. A-MEN.

2 Come, sing with us the praises
Of God's preserving care,
Who safe from harm has kept us
Throughout another year;
And crowned our lives with mercies
Unnumbered as the sand,
Which day by day have reached us
From His all-gracious hand.

3 Come, praise Him for the promise
Of strength in weakness given;
For means of grace provided,
For blessèd hope of heaven.
Oh, Christian youths and maidens!
Oh, brothers, old and young!
Uplift your hearts and voices,
And let His praise be sung. AMEN.

EASTER.

180. "THE WORLD ITSELF KEEPS EASTER DAY."

Contributed to this Hymnal by John A. Preston.

Allegro.

1. The world it-self keeps East-er Day, And East-er larks are sing-ing;
2. There stood three Ma-ries by the tomb On East-er morn-ing ear-ly,

And East-er flow'rs are bloom-ing gay, And East-er buds are spring-ing.
When day had scarce-ly chased the gloom, And dew was white and pearl-y.

The Lord hath ris'n, as all things tell: Good Christians, see ye rise as well!

Al-le-lu-ia, Al-le-lu-ia, Al-le - - - lu - - ia!

3 But earlier still the Angel sped,
His news of comfort giving;
And "Why," he said, "among the dead
Thus seek ye for the living?"
The Lord hath risen, etc.

4 The Church is keeping Easter Day,
And Easter hymns are sounding,
And Easter flowers are blooming gay,
The altar now surrounding.
The Lord hath risen, etc.

EASTER.

181. "YE HAPPY BELLS OF EASTER DAY."
Rev. J. S. B. Hodges.

1. Ye hap-py bells of East-er Day!
2. Ye glo-ry-bells of East-er Day!

Ring, ring your joy Thro' earth and sky! Ye ring a glo-rious word;
The hills that rise A-gainst the skies Re-ech-o with the word,—

The notes that swell in glad-ness tell The ris-ing of the Lord!
The vic-tor breath that con-quers Death,— The ris-ing of the Lord!

3 Ye passion-bells of Easter Day!
    The bitter cup
    He lifted up,
    Salvation to afford:
Ye saintly bells! your passion tells
    The rising of the Lord!

4 Ye victor bells of Easter Day!
    The thorny crown
    He layeth down:
Ring! ring! with strong accord,
The mighty strain of love and pain,—
    The rising of the Lord!

EASTER.

182. "THE BUDS ARE BURSTING ON THE TREES."

MABEL G. OSGOOD.   Composed for this Hymnal by R. H. CLOUSTON, Jr.

2 Come, let us all sweet blossoms bring
    The risen Lord to greet,
And make our hearts an offering,
    And lay them at his feet.
        Awake! etc.

3 No longer death and hopeless gloom
    Shall grieve our souls distressed;
For Christ has trodden, through the tomb,
    A pathway for the blest.
        Awake! etc.

EASTER.

183. "SWEETLY ARE THE BIRDS SINGING."

EMILY CHAPMAN. Composed for this Hymnal by R. H. CLOUSTON, Jr.

1. Sweet-ly are the birds sing-ing At East-er dawn; Sweet-ly are the bells ring-ing On East-er morn. And the words that they say, On this gladsome East-er day, Are "Christ the Lord is ris-en, is ris-en!"

2. Birds, oh ne'er for-get your sing-ing At East-er dawn! Bells, may ye be al-ways ring-ing On East-er morn! When the gloom-y night has gone, And this brightest day is born, Sing, "Christ the Lord is ris-en, is ris-en!"

3 Easter buds as now were growing
    Ages ago;
Easter lilies then were blooming
    By the waters' flow;
And in Nature all was bright,
Bathed in holy, radiant light,
For "Christ the Lord is risen, is risen!"

4 Buds, ye soon will turn to flowers,
    Cherry and white;
Storms of snow will change to showers,
    Darkness to light.
With the wakening of the spring,
Birds and flowers sweetly sing,
Lo, "Christ the Lord is risen, is risen!"

FLORAL.

184. ALL SEASONS. P. M.

1. Down in the valley, By the little rill, Where the merry brooklet flows, Never standing still,— There grow the vi-o-lets, There the May-flow'rs spring, Down beneath the wil-lows, Down where the waters sing. Spring-time comes to bring to me The violets blue 'neath the willow-tree,— Spring-time comes to bring to me The violets blue 'neath the willow-tree.

2. High on the hill-side, In the forest shade, Out upon the meadows green, Down within the glade,— There grow the lil-ies red, There the dai-sies grow, High up-on the hill-side, And in the meadows low. Sum-mer comes to bring to me The daisies bright on the sun-ny lea,— Sum-mer comes to bring to me The daisies bright on the sun-ny lea.

3 Out in the forest,
    Where the shadows green
Rest upon the mossy rocks,
    Sunny gleams between, —
There grows the golden-rod,
    Ere the asters die,
When the leaves are falling,
    And Autumn draweth nigh.
‖: Autumn comes to bring to me
The aster bright 'neath the leafless tree. :‖

4 Over the mountain,
    O'er the dreary hill,
Blossom out the flakes of snow
    Silently and still :
Strange winter blossoms they,
    Pure, and fair, and white,
Glowing in the sunbeams,
    Smiling in the light.
‖: Winter comes to bring to me
The snow-flake bloom o'er the land and sea. :‖

2 Oh, what so sweet as summer,
   When all the sky is blue,
And when the sunbeam's arrows
   Pierce all the green Earth through!
And what so sweet as flowers,
   The blossoms white and red,
Where troops of bright-wing'd insects
   Secure their daily bread!

3 Oh, what so sweet as birds are,
   That echo, in their trills,
The music of the summer winds,
   The murmur of the rills!
And all these sights and voices,
   In garden, field, and grove,
Make Earth, array'd in beauty,
   A type of God's own love.

FLORAL.

186. Rev. G. Blunt.   **OFFERTORY.**   11s & 10s.   Mary Palmer.

1. Here, Lord, we offer Thee all that is fairest,
Bloom from the garden, and flow'rs from the field;
Gifts for the stricken ones, knowing Thou carest
More for the love than the wealth that we yield. Amen.

2 Raise, Lord, to health again those who have sicken'd,
   Fair be their lives as the roses in bloom;
Give of Thy grace unto souls Thou hast quicken'd,
   Gladness for sorrow, and brightness for gloom.

3 We, Lord, like flowers, must bloom and must wither;
   We, like these blossoms, must fade and must die;
Gather us, Lord, to Thy presence forever,
   Grant us a place in the mansions on high. Amen.

NATIONAL.

187. COLUMBIA. 6.6.4.6.6.6.4.
Composed for this Hymnal by E. H. Bailey.

1. God bless our native land! Firm may she ever stand
Through storm and night! When the wild tempests rave,
Ruler of wind and wave, Do Thou our country save By Thy great might!

2 For her our pray'rs shall be,
Our fathers' God, to Thee:
On Thee we wait!
Be her walls Holiness;
Her rulers, Righteousness;
Her officers be Peace:
God save the State!

188. H. G. Spaulding. MEMORIAL. L. M. Martin Luther.

1. From land to land, to realms afar, Our Patriot He-ro's name has gone;
2. In Freedom's heirs still burn'd those fires Of patriot zeal, defying fate;

HARVEST.

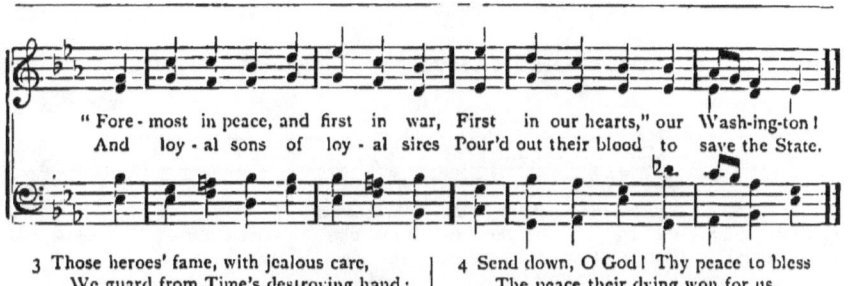

3 Those heroes' fame, with jealous care,
　We guard from Time's destroying hand;
Decay, that smites all else, shall spare
　Their memory who preserved our land.

4 Send down, O God! Thy peace to bless
　The peace their dying won for us,
Till over town and wilderness
　Extends Thy truth victorious.

189. WALTER N. EVANS.　　RUTH. 8s & 7s.

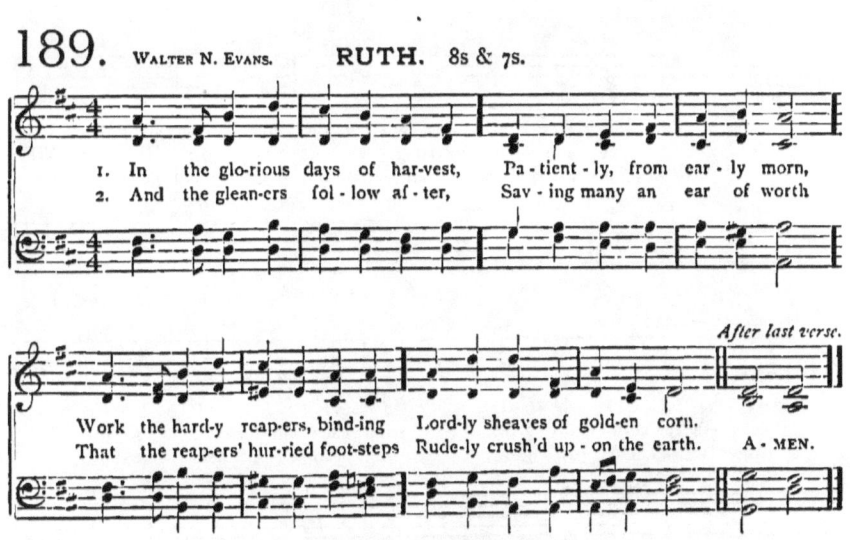

3 Gleaners we in life's great harvest;
　Seeking, in each lowly spot,
Tender grains of sweetest promise,
　By the reapers heeded not.

4 Every dark and hidden corner
　Of the boundless harvest-field,
Search'd with earnest, loving labor,
　Germs of noble life will yield.

5 And, when earthly days are ended,
　When the restful night is come,
We shall wake to share the glory
　Of our Father's "Harvest Home." AMEN.

HARVEST.

191. J. G. Whittier. THANKSGIVING. L. M. H. J. Gauntlett.

1. Once more the lib'-ral year laughs out O'er rich-er stores than gems or gold;
Once more with harvest song and shout Is Nature's bloodless triumph told.

2. Oh, fa-vors ev'-ry year made new! Oh, bless-ings with the sun-shine sent!
The boun-ty o-ver-runs our due, The fulness shames our dis-con-tent. A-MEN.

3 We shut our eyes, the flowers bloom on;
We murmur, but the corn-ears fill;
We choose the shadow, but the sun
That casts it shines behind us still.

4 Now let these altars, wreath'd with flowers
And piled with fruits, awake again
Thanksgiving for the golden hours,
The early and the latter rain! AMEN.

HARVEST.

192. "WE PLOUGH THE FERTILE MEADOWS."

German.

1. We plough the fer-tile mead-ows, We sow the fur-rowed land;
But all the growth and in-crease Are in God's might-y hand.
He gives the show'r and sun-shine To swell the quick'n-ing grain;
The spring-ing corn He bless-es, He clothes the gold-en plain.

2 He only is the Maker
  Of all things near and far,
He forms the earth and ocean,
  He kindles every star;
His love ordains the seasons,
  By Him are all things fed:
He for the sparrow careth,
  He gives our daily bread.

3 All praise to Thee, our Father,
  Thou giver of all good;
Upon whose care dependeth
  Our life and health and food;
We bring our glad thanksgiving,
  Our gifts of love and praise;
Be Thine our grateful service,
  The harvest of our days.

HARVEST.

193. "THE CORN IS RIPE FOR REAPING."

1. The corn is ripe for reap-ing, Fields glow with rud-dy grain,
   And we must now be keep-ing Our har-vest feast a-gain;
   With voice of joy and sing-ing, Our praise to God shall rise,
   Who, whilst the seed was spring-ing, Rain'd bless-ings from the skies.

2. Thine, Fa-ther, is the riv-er That mak-eth rich the earth;
   Thro' Thee, O Gra-cious Giv-er, The bur-ied seed had birth:
   Thou on the fur-rows rain-ing, Didst make them soft with show'rs,
   The thirst-y crops main-tain-ing Thro' si-lent sum-mer hours. A-MEN.

3 The year, by Thee anointed,
    Is now with goodness crowned;
  Robed in the robes appointed,
    With gladness girded round.
  We thank Thee for the blessing
    Which meets us on our way,
  And come, Thy love confessing,
    With happy hearts to-day.

4 But whilst our lips are praising,
    Our lives to Thee belong;
  With them we would be raising
    A nobler, sweeter song;
  One that may sound forever,
    Whilst earth's great Harvest speeds,—
  A song of high endeavor
    Rung out in earnest deeds.' AMEN.

CHRISTMAS.

194. "THE DAY THAT CHRIST WAS BORN."

1. Ring, ring the bells, the joy-ful bells, This mer-ry Christmas morn! Their sweet, me-lo-dious mu-sic tells The day that Christ was born. Sweet-ly they sound o'er vale and glen, Hark! how their mu-sic swells With "Peace on earth, good-will to men!" O mer-ry Christmas bells! Ring, ring the bells, the Christmas bells, The bells, the mer-ry, mer-ry Christ-mas bells!

The bells

2 Ring, ring the bells, the Christmas bells!
  For, in their joyous chime,
Once more on earth the chorus swells
  Of angel song sublime.
The sweet old story, ever new,
  Falls on the heart again, —
Refreshing as the early dew,
  Or the soft summer rain.
    Ring, ring, etc.

3 Ring, ring the bells, the Christmas bells!
  Prophetic of the day
When he of whom their music tells
  Shall all the nations sway;
Shall bless and fill and rule each heart,
  Shall bid all sorrows cease;
And give his own the better part
  Of everlasting peace.
    Ring, ring, etc.

CHRISTMAS.

195. "RING, CHRISTMAS BELLS!"

S. N. MITCHELL. R. H. CLOUSTON, Jr.

Allegretto. To be sung in unison.

1. Ring, Christmas bells, ring merrily, And herald in the morn! Ring in with carols cheerily The day that Christ was born!

2. Our Far, far away, in Palestine, He saw the light of day, And 'neath the Star of Bethlehem, Within a manger lay.

2 Ring, Christmas bells, ring merrily,
　　And peal your sweetest chime!
　Ring in the day with tones of joy
　　And sweet melodious rhyme!
　Our Saviour, Christ, was born to-day;
　　No pillow eased his head,
　His cradle was a manger hard,
　　Wherein the cattle fed.

3 Ring, Christmas bells, ring merrily,
　　And sweetest accents give!
　Our blessed Saviour, Jesus, died,
　　That we might truly live.
　Upon the cross his spirit fled
　　When he was crucified,
　And now, within his home on high,
　　He bids us all abide.

From Russell's "Musical Library," by permission of J. M. Russell, owner of copyright.

CHRISTMAS.

196. "CAROL, CAROL, CHRISTIANS!"

Composed for this Hymnal by H. G. SPAULDING.

CHRISTMAS.

198. BETHLEHEM. P. M.

Rev. Phillips Brooks, D.D.   L. H. Redner.

1. O little town of Bethlehem, How still we see thee lie!
   Above thy deep and dreamless sleep The silent stars go by;
   Yet in thy dark streets shineth The everlasting Light;
   The hopes and fears of all the years Are met in thee to-night!

2. For Christ is born of Mary; And gathered all above,
   While mortals sleep, the angels keep Their watch of wond'ring love.
   O morning stars! together Proclaim the holy birth,
   And praises sing to God the King, And peace to men on earth! A-MEN.

After last verse.

3 How silently, how silently
   The wondrous gift is given!
So God imparts to human hearts
   The blessings of His heaven.
No ear may hear his coming;
   But in this world of sin,
Where meek souls will receive him still,
   The dear Christ enters in.

4 O holy Child of Bethlehem!
   Descend to us, we pray;
Cast out our sin and enter in,—
   Be born in us to-day!
We hear the Christmas angels
   The great glad tidings tell,—
Oh, come to us, abide with us,
   Our Lord Emmanuel! Amen.

INDEX OF FIRST LINES

In the Hymnal.

	Hymn
A band of youthful pilgrims	82
Abide with me! fast falls the eventide	169
Above the clear blue sky	17
Again the Lord of life and light	27
All my heart this night rejoices	197
And now this hour of praise	35
Angels holy, high and lowly	52
Another week's campaign is o'er	39
Art thou weary?	88
As a bird in meadow fair	119
As helpless as a child who clings	61
Behold the Prince of Peace	105
Beneath the shadow of the cross	87
Be not swift to take offence	157
Carol, carol, Christians	196
Come, brothers, let us go!	152
Come, Christian youths and maidens	179
Come forth and bring your garlands	185
Come, friends! the world wants mending	151
Come, happy children!	8
Come, labor on!	138
Deal gently with us, Lord!	125
Down in the valley	184
Ever would we fain be reading	90
Every gentle gale that blows	50
Every morn the red sun	163
Fair waved the golden corn	62
Father, again to Thy dear name we raise	33
Father, blessed Father!	81
Father, from Thy throne on high	72
Father, from Thy throne on high	76
Father, hear the prayer we offer!	71
Father, let me henceforth be	64

	Hymn
Father, let Thy benediction	77
Father, Thy boundless love	122
Father, to Thee we look in all our sorrow	164
Father, we are young and weak	135
Feeble, helpless, how shall I	106
Fierce raged the tempest o'er the deep	100
"Follow me," the Master said	95
"Forever with the Lord!"	168
For life and health we bless Thee, Lord	12
For the beauty of the earth	47
Forth to the fight, ye faithful	83
Forward! be our watchword	84
Framer of the light	7
From land to land, to realms afar	188
Gird Thou our souls, O God of might!	143
God bless our native land!	187
God is in the heavens above us	58
God is love! His mercy brightens	48
God make my life a little light	78
God of heaven, O hear us singing!	176
God of Jesus, hear me now	101
God of mercy and of love	63
God, who madest earth and heaven	40
God will take care of you	109
Hail, sacred day of earthly rest	29
Hail the Cross of Jesus!	96
Hail, thou bright and sacred morn	32
Hark, hark, my soul!	118
Hark! round the God of love	75
Hark! the loving Saviour's voice	102
Have mercy, O our Father!	133
Have ye looked for my sheep in the desert	104
Hear us, Heavenly Father	65
Hear ye not a voice from heaven	111
Heavenly Shepherd, true and holy	15
Heaven's arches rang when the angels sang	98

INDEX OF FIRST LINES.

First line	Hymn
He cometh not a king to reign	89
He hides within the lily	45
Here, Lord, we offer Thee all that is fairest	186
Higher, higher, will we climb	121
Holy, holy, holy Lord God Almighty!	9
Holy offerings rich and rare	73
I have a Father up in heaven	23
I hear a sweet voice ringing clear	110
I heard the voice of Jesus say	97
I know, O Father, all my life	123
I little see, I little know	129
I need Thy presence, Lord, each passing hour	126
In hearts from sin delivered	144
In the cross of Christ I glory	94
In the glorious days of harvest	189
In this peaceful hour of prayer	30
I sing the mighty power of God	49
I thank Thee, Lord, that Thou hast made	114
I think, when I read that sweet story of old	103
It singeth low in every heart	162
I would, dear Jesus, I could break	91
Lead us, Heavenly Father	68
Let us sing! — the angels sing	3
Life is not a fleeting shadow	141
Life is onward, — use it	146
Little by little the time goes by	139
Little hands, be free in giving	175
Looking upward every day	36
Lord, this day Thy children meet	31
Lord, Thy children guide and keep	120
Lord, Thy glory fills the heaven	2
Lord, Thy word abideth	112
Lord, what offerings shall we bring?	159
Maker of all things, loving all Thy creatures	11
More love, O God, to Thee	131
Nearer, my God, to Thee	132
Never lose the golden rule	153
Now to our loving Father, God	19
O'er the wide and restless ocean	137
O Father! by Thy holy will	167
O Father of mercies! Thy praises here we sing	1
Oft have I walked the woodland paths	56
O God! our help in ages past	170
O God, whose presence glows in all	18
Oh, day of rest and gladness!	25
Oh, lead me, my Father, lead Thou, lest I stray!	134
Oh, the Father's hands are helping	117
Oh, valiant little soldiers	85
Oh, worship the King, all glorious above!	6
O little birds that all day long	67
O little town of Bethlehem	198
O Lord of heaven, and earth, and sea	14
O Lord, while angels praise Thee	5
O Love! O Life! our faith and sight	93
Once more the liberal year laughs out	191
Once more to Thee, O Father	16
One by one the sands are flowing	149
One gift, my God, I seek	127
One sweetly solemn thought	166
One thought I have, my ample creed	115
On our way rejoicing	38
Onward, Christian soldiers	79
Onward, onward, though the region	148
O Paradise! O Paradise!	165
O sweet Sabbath bells!	28
Our Father, bless us ere we go	37
Pleasant are Thy courts above	107
Praise the Lord! who reigns above	24
Raise a glad and grateful song	158
Rescue the perishing, bring home the wanderers	154
Ring, Christmas bells, ring merrily	195
Ring, ring the bells, the joyful bells	194
See the rivers flowing	160
Singing, the reapers homeward come	190
Sing praise to God for sun and shade	69
Songs of praise the angels sang	4
Speak gently! it is better far	150
Speak the truth! for that is right	155
Strive! yet I do not promise	140
Strong in the living God	142
Sunny days of childhood!	70
Sun of my soul, forever near	128
Sweet is the task, O Lord	22
Sweetly are the birds singing	183
The buds are bursting on the trees	182
The child leans on its parent's breast	124
The corn is ripe for reaping	193
The days are gliding swiftly by	44
The ever-changing seasons	178
The fields are all white	174
The freshly blooming flowers	54

INDEX OF FIRST LINES.

	Hymn
The harp at Nature's advent strung	43
The heavens declare His glory	51
The Lord is in His Holy Place	116
The Master hath come, and he calls us to follow	92
The morning, the bright and the beautiful morning	20
There are lonely hearts to cherish	156
There is a book, who runs may read	42
There 's music in the midnight breeze	57
There lives a voice within me	136
The sweetest name in heaven above	66
The world is bright and fair, we know	161
The world itself keeps Easter Day	180
The world looks very beautiful	86
This is the day of light	26
Thou art, O God, the life and light	55
Thou knowest, Lord, the weariness and sorrow	108
Thou, Lord of life, whose tender care	130
Thou One in all, Thou All in one!	13
To and fro! to and fro!	177
We are but pilgrims here	171
We are children of one Father	21
We come in childhood's innocence	74
We come, O God, with gladness	60
We plough the fertile meadows	192
We thank Thee, Lord, for this fair earth	46
What can little ones like me	173
Whate'er my God ordains is right	113
What is birdie doing	172
"What is the law of thy beauty?"	53
When morning gilds the skies	10
When the day of life is dawning	99
When the nightfall round us closes	41
When this song of praise shall cease	34
Whither are you going?	80
Who is on the Lord's side?	147
Work, for the night is coming	145
Ye happy bells of Easter Day!	181
Yes, God is good: in earth and sky	59

www.ingramcontent.com/pod-product-compliance
Lightning Source LLC
Chambersburg PA
CBHW032118230426
43672CB00009B/1779